ACCLAIM FOR
Parenting for Eternity

"Dear family, from the very outset—the dedication Conor Gallagher wrote for his book (I won't give a spoiler)—to its conclusion, Mr. Gallagher's words are so full of Grace that your heart cannot but be moved to the core. I'll put my money where my mouth is—I'm getting every one of my parishioners a copy because this book is priceless. It is priceless because your child's soul is priceless. Praise be to God and thanks be to Conor Gallagher for—well, there are no words, just no words, for the Grace you will find inside."

—*Fr. James Altman, Pastor of St. James*
the Less Catholic Parish, La Crosse,
Wisconsin

"In his latest work, Conor Gallagher stirs a generation of parents from the hypnotic trance of the modern world with an awakening to their children's eternal destiny. Drawing from Scripture, the saints, and the masters in the spiritual life, as well as his own experiences as a father of fourteen,

Gallagher offers parents a beautiful guide to keeping their children on the narrow road to Heaven. *Parenting for Eternity* is a book all parents should read—and then re-read—as they undertake the greatest mission (and blessing) God has given us: to get our children to Heaven."

—*Carrie Gress, author of* The Anti-Mary Exposed *and* Theology of Home

"Like many, I enjoy books filled with hard-hitting truths. But just because the truth is clear doesn't mean living it is easy, and this is especially true in the home. Keeping our eyes fixed on both eternity and the good of our family can be a real challenge, one made harder by our endless distractions. Gallagher, as a Catholic father, offers the kind of wisdom that only comes from a deep love of truth steeped in real and raw experience. I can't recommend it enough."

—*Jason Craig, husband, father, author, and co-founder of Fraternus*

PARENTING

for

Eternity

*A Guide to Raising Children
in Holy Mother Church*

CONOR GALLAGHER

TAN BOOKS
GASTONIA, NORTH CAROLINA

Scripture citations are from the Douay-Rheims 1899 American Edition.

Cover design by www.davidferrisdesign.com

Cover image: Paradiso, Canto 31: Illustration from 'The Divine Comedy' by Dante Alighieri, by Gustave Doré, 1832 - 1883, French / Photo © Giancarlo Costa / Bridgeman Images

Library of Congress Control Number: 2021932155

ISBN: 978-1-5051-2107-0
Kindle ISBN: 978-1-5051-2108-7
ePUB ISBN: 978-1-5051-2109-4

Published in the United States by
TAN Books
PO Box 269
Gastonia, NC 28053
www.TANBooks.com

Printed in India

To my miscarried children:
I am sorry I do not think of you more often. Intercede for me,
that I may one day embrace you with a father's love.

CONTENTS

PREFACE

Dear Reader,

I, your unworthy author, must emphasize two points before you begin this little book on parenting. The first is in regard to the style of the work, and the second is a vital disclaimer.

Regarding style: I have adopted a rather antiquated style of writing for this work. Spiritual writers of old spoke directly to the reader with phrases like "Christian Reader" or "Immortal Soul" or even "Unworthy Christian." Modern sensitivities emphasize the first-person plural pronouns of "we" and "us" in an unnecessary attempt to avoid the appearance of paternalism or arrogance. So when I address "you," as the reader, I am truly saying "we," for the message of this book is intended for myself as much as anyone.

Additionally, my favorite works of spirituality have a very particular voice: a voice that calls the reader to conversion, as if the author has but one page . . . one paragraph . . . one single sentence to convert the reader to Jesus Christ. Such a voice is starkly different from an intellectual work intended to convince the reader's mind of a superior argument. Here, I hope to jar your soul to conversion with the power and beauty of truth—particularly the truth that your child will live for trillions and trillions of years in either glory or damnation and that you, Dear Parent, are the primary educator of this immortal soul.

Now, a vital disclaimer: I beg you, remember that preaching and doing are two different things. Yes, I am a parent of fourteen living children at the moment, but I fail horrifically at many of the precepts in this work, and writing it has been an examination of conscience, convicting me of my need for a lifetime of conversion and reparation.

In conclusion, here is the goal of this work in a nutshell: *that you, Christian Parent, look upon your child as an immortal creature.* I believe that if we truly focused on the notion of eternity, our parenting would radically change for the better.

Sincerely Yours,
Conor Gallagher

INTRODUCTION

Look at your little child. See the little smile, the little nose; see the little arms and legs; hear the sweet little voice that calls your name in joy and sorrow. If you could, you would imitate God and number the hairs upon your little one's head (see Mt 10:30), treasuring each one, "for where your treasure is, there will your heart be also" (Lk 12:34).

You will move Heaven and earth for those little limbs and little hairs—those things that were made from dust, "and into dust [they] shalt return" (Gn 3:19).

But that little soul! That little soul shall never return to dust. It shall, God willing, forever rejoice before the splendor of all that is good, true, and beautiful, reveling in inexplicable joy, overcome with inexhaustible glory, relishing every moment more and more for eternity, never slowing, never tiring, never ceasing, and never exhausting the infinity of the Beatific Vision.

Or that little soul—if it be a child of the kingdom of man (see Mt 8:12)—will suffer the threats of Jesus Christ: "The Son of man shall send his angels, and they shall gather out of his kingdom all scandals, and them that work iniquity. And shall cast them into the furnace of fire: there shall be weeping and gnashing of teeth" (Mt 13: 41–42).

Imagine, your little one surrounded with unquenchable lust and wrath. It is hard to imagine. In fact, you might find it easier to imagine a child locked in a dark cellar, abused and malnourished by the cursed hand of a demonic man. Some such children live to tell their stories. And your heart plummets to your stomach, sickened with sympathy, so grateful your child has been spared from such a plight.

But such a plight is nothing compared to the pit of Satan's lair, where every light of hope and love is extinguished.

How foolish we are! If your sweet little one had cancer, suffering the pangs of chemotherapy, needles, and fear of the unknown—if your little daughter's head was bald and covered with scarves or your son no longer had the strength to throw a ball—you would rightly move Heaven and earth to save your child's body with the most innovative treatment; you would, without hesitation, work a second shift, or even beg for money from family, friends, and strangers; you would expose your own sorrow and plead for mercy from your creditors; you would cease to care about your own health, wealth, and reputation; your personal dreams would gladly be abandoned and replaced with one simple dream of holding your child's broken body in your arms one more day. You would, indeed, die a thousand deaths to salvage your child's one life.

But you must confront the following question with scrutiny and sincerity: how much of this paternal affection do you direct toward your little one's soul? All your efforts to save the little heart that pumps blood, but so little effort to save the soul that lives forever. How often have you darted across the room to save your toddler from ingesting a dangerous chemical but shrugged your shoulders at the impurity on streaming video or the wrath on video games? How often have you sat on pins and needles awaiting your new driver to return home safely but think little about his soul crashing into the dregs of humanity on his smartphone? The mere thought of a man violating your teenager daughter is too much to bear, yet you hardly consider the kings of pop culture infecting her with their own moral code. "And fear ye not them that kill the body, and are not able to kill the soul: but rather fear him that can destroy both soul and body in hell" (Mt 10:28).

As a parent, you must examine your conscience: do you give greater attention to your child's physical or spiritual well-being? Have you gone to great lengths to construct your entire life around your child's health, education, social life, and sports so they can be well-rounded, productive, and successful citizens? A resounding yes comes to mind. But have you given even 10 percent of such effort to their spiritual formation? Have you considered Heaven and hell 10 percent as much as you consider worldly success for your growing child? Perhaps you regret not having the resources to pay for college, travel, or family vacations. But do you regret not taking your child to Eucharistic Adoration and confession and helping him fall deeply—madly—in love with Our Lady?

As a parent, you must dwell upon the day of your judgment, standing on trial before the throne of God, with all the angels and saints gazing upon you and the evidence laid before the Supreme Judge. And the angelic choirs will sing out the divine teaching of the God-man: "It were better for him, that a millstone were hanged about his neck, and he cast into the sea, than that he should scandalize one of these little ones" (Lk 17:2). That is right! Your little ones. Almighty God has given you care of innocent babes who are like "sheep in the midst of wolves" (Mt 10:16), whom the devil, like "a roaring lion," prowls about seeking to devour (1 Pt 5:8).

As a loving father or mother, you must do everything to get your child to Heaven. Yet due to the effects of original sin (darkness of intellect, weakness of will, and proneness to evil), your eyes remain fixed on this mortal coil we call earth. It is only through grace that you can be freed from the chains of your senses, enabling you to transcend earthly fixation, focusing all your thoughts, emotions, and grit on your child's eternal glory.

Fear not if you are unqualified to lead your child on the path of righteousness! Take heart in the fact that Noah got drunk, Moses had a speech impediment, David was a murderer and adulterer, Peter was a coward, Thomas was a doubter, Paul was a persecutor—and Lazarus was dead. For the Lord told St. Paul, "My grace is sufficient for thee; for power is made perfect in infirmity" (2 Cor 12:9). With grace, Dear Parent, teach your child that which you do not yet fully possess, for God uses broken vessels to accomplish His will. And, therefore, oh flawed and weak parent, be like St. Paul and say to yourself, "Gladly therefore will I glory in my infirmities, that the power of Christ may dwell in me" (12:9).

Despite the litany of sins casting a shadow over the light of your baptismal grace, if you focus on the smallest truths and perform the simplest acts of devotion, the glory of God's brilliant light will burst forth onto your children, lighting the path to their very own mansion awaiting them in the Father's house (see Jn 14:2).

In this little book, you will read about those little truths and simple devotions that are sufficient for forming your child's conscience so that he will have the strength necessary

St. Peter Denying Christ

to shun the kingdom of man and every opportunity to become an eternal resident of the kingdom of God.

Dear Reader, if you believe these profound truths and lead your family in these simple devotions, you will one day be able to repeat the Canticle of Simeon, a hymn proclaimed by an old, tired, but vigilant man awaiting the Messiah in the Temple. He lovingly took the baby Jesus from the Virgin Mother into his own arms. He held that innocent child and gazed into His eyes with love and affection, just as you do with your own. He looked up at Heaven and proclaimed the very words that every parent ought to declare with their own dying breath, knowing that they as parents have done the will of God: "Now thou dost dismiss thy servant, O Lord, according to thy word in peace" (Lk 2:29).

THE FOUR LAST
THINGS FIRST

Death

There is perhaps no more counterintuitive notion for a parent than this: *you must prepare your child for death.*[1] From the moment you learned of your child in the womb, you have directed all your God-given instincts, your energy, and passion into keeping that child alive. You would move mountains to keep your son healthy; you would suffer any pain to free your daughter from her own. You have reared the little one for a happy and long life and perhaps prayed the parent's prayer: *Dearest Lord, please allow my child to outlive me.* Yes, you have been preparing your child for living!

The modern world treats death as a thing of horror. And in a sense, it is. "Now why is death so hard, so terrible a

---

[1]   See Alphonsus Liguori, *Preparation for Death* (Charlotte, NC: TAN Books, 1982).

thing? It is because the soul has to separate itself from the body. Body and soul were created for each other, and so intimate is their union that a parting between them seems almost impossible. They would endure almost anything rather than be torn asunder."[2] This is a natural response, so natural that Our Lord experienced inconceivable agony at the hour of His death, not just because of the nails piercing His hands and feet, but due to the horror of the separation of body and soul:

> We know from the testimony of our Redeemer Himself that no agony is like the agony of death. Although through the whole course of His sorrowful passion, He was tortured in a terrible manner, yet all the martyrdom He endured was not to be compared with what He suffered at the moment of His death. This we gather from the Gospels. Nowhere do we find that at any period of His life the greatness of the pains He bore extorted from Our Lord a cry of anguish. But when the moment came for Him to expire, and the ruthless hand of death rent His Heart asunder, we read that He cried out with a loud voice, and gave up his ghost.[3]

Thus, even the most faithful of our children will likely have a horror of death, and rightly so. After all, death is

---

2   Martin von Cochem, *The Four Last Things* (Charlotte, NC: TAN Books, 2015), p. 2.

3   Ibid., p. 3.

a horrible thing in itself, the last enemy to be destroyed (see 1 Cor 15:26). It is the punishment of Adam's rebellion against God: "And he commanded him, saying: 'Of every tree of paradise thou shalt eat: But of the tree of knowledge of good and evil, thou shalt not eat. For in what day soever thou shalt eat of it, *thou shalt die the death*" (Gn 2:16–17; emphasis added).

The secular world, however, adds an additional fear to death: an unhealthy fear, a godless fear. To the unfaithful, death is seen as the end rather than the beginning; death is seen as failure rather than completion; death is to be raged against with every fiber of your living body. As the Welsh poet Dylan Thomas so aptly put, "Do not go gentle into that good night. / Rage, rage against the dying of the light."[4] And this is exactly what the modern man does, for he does not believe that God waits for him on the other side. Imagine this lack of faith added to the natural horror of separation of body and soul!

---

[4]   The first and last stanza are a good summary of the poem:
       Do not go gentle into that good night,
       Old age should burn and rave at close of day;
       Rage, rage against the dying of the light.
       . . .
       And you, my father, there on the sad height,
       Curse, bless, me now with your fierce tears, I pray.
       Do not go gentle into that good night.
       Rage, rage against the dying of the light.

St. Peter waged a similar protest to Christ's own passion and death. As parents, we must hear Our Lord's reprimand: "Go behind me, Satan, thou art a scandal unto me: because thou savourest not the things that are of God, but the things that are of men" (Mt 16:23).

The eyes of faith—the eyes of a truly loving parent—see death as the glorious gateway to eternal life. Truly, the horror will present itself. But that does not mean it must be met without hope.

Despite its complete contrariness to modern sentiments, another stark reality of death is this: the demonic will assault your child upon his death more so than they ever did during life. St. Gregory the Great says, "Consider well how terrible is the hour of death, and how appalling the remembers of evil deeds will be at that time. For the spirits of darkness will recall all the harm they have done us, and remind us of the sins which we have committed at their instigation. *They will not go to the death-bed of the godless only, but they will be present with the elect, striving to discover something sinful whereof they accuse them.*"[5]

There is, however, an antidote to this terror: reliance on the Blessed Mother at the hour of our death. We will address her later, but for now, note this: the Hail Mary says, "Pray for us now and at the hour of our death."

---

[5]   Martin von Cochem, *The Four Last Things*, p. 8; emphasis added.

Dear Parent, do the following math: if your child is ten years of age and were to pray the Holy Rosary every day until death at age eighty, how many times would he have implored the Blessed Virgin to intercede for him at the moment of death? There are fifty-three Hail Marys in every Rosary. If they prayed fifty-three Hail Marys every year 365 times, that is 19,345. Multiply that by seventy years. *That is 1,354,150 times!* What better way can you prepare your child for a holy death than by praying the Rosary daily? If your little one implores the Mother of God over one million times to be present with him at the hour of death, do you think she will ignore him? And those demons—all the forces of hell—have no power over the Blessed Virgin. God told Satan in the Garden of Eden, "I will put enmities between thee and the woman, and thy seed and her seed: she shall crush thy head, and thou shalt lie in wait for her heel" (Gn 3:15). With Mary's help, the demons stalking your child at his death will be met by Mary's heel. Please take this to heart, and never go another night without praying the Rosary with your little one.

In the truest light of reality, you must help your child see that death is God's way to bring us to our eternal home. While we should not be fatalistic or dwell too heavily on the subject with little ones, we should also never hide this ultimate reality from them. It requires clear and clever thinking on the part of parents to communicate the truths of the Faith, including the inevitability of death.

Countless opportunities present themselves to cover such a topic with a child. Death is all around, even for a youngster. The flowers will wilt; the leaves will fall; pets will perish; grandparents will pass—perhaps quickly, perhaps slowly. A child must see that death is part of life and that we were not made for this world.

Dear Parent, teach your child that St. Joseph is the patron saint of a happy death, for he died in the arms of Jesus Christ and the Blessed Mother. Your child will die as he has lived. And you have the unique ability to instill in his little soul a desire for a happy death in those sacred arms that held good St. Joseph. Zealously prepare your child for a happy death by first living a holy life.

The greatest gift you can give your child is not that which you provide during your life but what you provide him long after you are gone. Your voice can sound in his mind, many years from now, as he lays dying: "Reach out for the Blessed Mother and Jesus Christ. They will take you to God the Father."

Judgment

Bring the powers of your imagination to bear: your adorable, sweet baby matures into a young man who unpredictably commits a wicked crime despite all your efforts to raise him as an honorable citizen. You once clothed him in cute overalls, dressed him in a fine suit for his first Communion, helped him buy his first suit and tie for a homecoming dance, and even straightened his bow tie on his wedding day. And now he wears an orange jumpsuit with a chilling prisoner number on his back. You once taught the little one to walk, caught him when he stumbled, and put his first little shoes on his tiny feet. You patiently taught him to tie his shoes. You showed your little man how to polish his shoes—and even how to dance. But now you hear the clanking of shackles around his ankles as you watch him shuffle little steps like a child learning to walk again. And those little hands that once covered the walls with finger painting, that reached up and held your own as you walked through a busy parking lot—the little hands you taught to make the sign of the cross—are now bound in handcuffs. In the eyes of the world, your little one is a criminal, deserving of a lifetime of loneliness and isolation, removed from all that is good and holy. Imagine the fate that awaits your beloved son: a cold, sterile room, surrounded by other vile criminals that do not care for your little one but will use and abuse him for an unbearable time. And you, as father and mother, can no longer protect him. You cannot take those little hands and lead him to safety. Your time is over. Everything in life you care about is dehumanized and shackled, helplessly guilty before a judge. All that you love is in the judge's hands and his alone.

Visualizing such a moment might send shivers down your spine. Perhaps you even find it unfair for the author to put such an unforgiving image in your mind. Perhaps you find it even absurd. And yet, what you may or may not know is that your little one *has* committed a wicked crime. It is called a venial sin. And the judge is Almighty God.

If you consider these words about venial sin as mere hyperbole, consider the piercing reminder of St. John Henry Newman: "[The Catholic Church] holds that it were better for sun and moon to drop from Heaven, for the earth to fail, and for all the many millions who are upon it to die of starvation in extremest agony, as far as temporal affliction goes, than that one soul, I will not say, should be lost, but should commit one single venial sin, should tell one wilful untruth . . . or steal one poor farthing without excuse."[6]

As a sinner myself, and as a parent of many adorable sinners, I am tempted to deafen my ears to the Church's authority, the voice of the saints, and the great minds that have grappled with sin and judgment for two thousand years. But upon reflection, shall I really conclude that I know better than all the wise souls before me? Shall I really conclude that sin is not as horrid as these brilliant and

---

[6]   John Henry Newman, *Lectures on Anglican Difficulties* (1852), Lecture 8.

saintly men and women have claimed? Pride has one goal: to lessen my fear of judgment.

Scripture is filled with holy men and women quaking in fear of judgment. The great King David, the man after God's own heart, declared, "Enter not into judgment with thy servant: for in thy sight no man living shall be justified" (Ps 142:2). And Job, a man who knew suffering better than us all, said, "What shall I do if God arises to judge me? What am I that I should answer Him? I cannot answer Him one for a thousand."

God's judgment is a heavy subject. But is not worldly judgment also a weighty topic? As a good lawyer prepares his client for what is to come before the tribunal, so too can a solid parenting book help you prepare your little one for particular judgment. Father Martin von Cochem provides six reasons that "strike terror into the soul when she is summoned to the particular judgment."

1. The soul fears because she knows her Judge to be omniscient;[7] that nothing can be concealed from Him, nor can He be in any way deceived.
2. Because her Judge is omnipotent;[8] nothing can withstand Him, and no one can escape from Him.

---

[7] Omniscient means *all-knowing*. We cannot hide from God, as Adam and Eve foolishly tried to do in the garden (see Gn 3:8).

[8] Omnipotent means *all powerful*.

3. Because her Judge is not merely the most just, but the most strict of judges, to whom sin is so hateful that He will not allow the slightest transgression to pass unpunished.

4. Because the soul knows that God is not her judge alone, but also her accuser; she has provoked Him to anger, she has offended Him, and He will defend His honor and avenge every insult offered to it.

5. Because the soul is aware that the sentence once uttered is irrevocable and there is no appeal for her to a higher court, it is useless for her to complain of the sentence. It cannot be reversed, and whether adverse or favorable she must accept it.

6. The most powerful reason of all why the soul fears to appear before the judgment seat is because she knows not what the sentence of the Judge will be. She has far more cause to fear than to hope. And all thought of help is now over—forever, forever lost; forever, forever damned![9]

Yes, Dear Parent, strike the fear of judgment into your child's soul, but *never, never* for ghoulish or melancholic

---

reasons. Rather, you must remind your child of judgment so that he not only knows but *feels* the eternal consequence of his actions. Your child, due to his original sin, makes the horrible mistake of seeing his actions as contained to this world. But our heavenly Father has given your little one an earthly father and mother to correct this error. Just as you so lovingly teach your child the long-term consequences of diet, education, and good and bad friendships, you must persistently plead with him to see the eternal consequence of *every single action.*

Dear Parent, hear me: nothing escapes God's watchful eye. Everything your little one ever does is inscribed into the eternal Judge's ledger.[10] And to allow your son or daughter to ever think anything else, I dare say, is child abuse.

Hell

In the book entitled *The Dogma of Hell: Illustrated by Facts Taken From Profane and Sacred History*, Father F. X. Schouppe, SJ, begins as crisply as any author could make it: "THE DOGMA OF HELL is the most terrible truth of our faith. There *is* a Hell. We are as sure of it as of the existence of God, the existence of the sun. Nothing, in fact,

---

[10]   The exception to this is the cleansing of your little one's soul in the sacrament of confession, which will be discussed in a later chapter.

is more clearly revealed than the dogma of Hell, *and Jesus Christ proclaims it as many as fifteen times in the Gospel.*"[11]

To deny your child a keen awareness of the reality of hell is one of the greatest neglects possible. What would you think of a parent who does not teach his son about the dangers of wild dogs next door? Or a parent who never warns his teenage daughter about walking through dark alleys at night?

Of course, you do not want your little one fearing the world to the point of seclusion. But a healthy fear of the world's dangers is always appropriate.

And what of the greatest threat to your child? What of eternal damnation? Surely, it is tempting to belittle the notion because you are raising a law-abiding citizen. You are not raising a monster, an animal, a hostile enemy of the Lord. This, Dear Parent, may be the very thought that leads you to the sin of presumption.

No! Train your child to work with diligence to avoid hell. Tell your child to prove to God every day that he fears hell by avoiding sin at all costs; tell him to beg for God's mercy to be admitted to Heaven. This is not morbid. This is true.

---

[11] F. X. Schouppe, *The Dogma of Hell: Illustrated by Facts Taken from Profane and Sacred History* (Charlotte, NC: TAN Books, 2012), p. 1; emphasis added. A complete list of these fifteen warnings is provided in appendix 1.

No one should grow up in a morbid and joyless home. When parents focus too much on the darkness, they tend to smother the light. Finding the right level of emphasis is difficult. But one way is to teach your child that the dogma of hell is in accordance with God's love! And this seemingly counterintuitive concept requires much effort and many years of instruction.

God's infinite love does not force your child to love Him. His love provides free will. We *choose* hell.

There is a danger, however, of taking the notion to an extreme. Do not believe that a person must stand up as a Satanist and proclaim his desire for eternal torment. No! Hell comes much easier than that, as Christ's warnings in those fifteen passages prove.

Consider reading those fifteen warnings to your family, one by one. Discuss each one. Jesus must have thought it important to state the same truth with such creativity and frequency.

As your child grows older, consider giving him books on the many apparitions of hell. Help him to avoid a morbid interest but still appreciate the reality that God has granted us insights into the inferno.

In the end, hell is a very disturbing truth, but it is also a sign of God's justice and love, for what good father does not warn his children of danger beforehand? Many souls have been saved due to their fear of hell. And the same goes

for your own child. A healthy fear of Satan and his domin-
ion is, in fact, a grace from God. But ultimately, however,
the greater fear should be the loss of Heaven. Such a fear
is more worthy of a holy man or woman. And it is now
Heaven to which we turn.

Heaven

It is far too easy for you to say you desire Heaven for your
child. It is so easy to say that it becomes almost meaning-
less. It behooves us to stop and think deeply—very deeply—about the subject of Paradise for your child.

Take your mind back to the moment you learned that
you were a parent. As mother, did you take a pregnancy
test at home? As father, did you receive a phone call, a text,
a special note? What were the first thoughts that occupied
your mind? Did you think finances? Were you out of wed-
lock and ashamed? Was it an answer to prayer after many
years of yearning for a child?

But ask yourself: how much of your thinking was
self-centered? Did you realize at the time that an immortal
soul was just discovered, a soul that had the potential to
spend eternity in Paradise with the King of kings? Would
you have been more excited about discovering a winning
lotto ticket in your coat pocket?

And did you feel the weightiness of *your* sudden responsibility to the little one? Did you realize that if you were lackadaisical in forming your child in the Faith that Jesus Christ would vomit you from His mouth (see Rv 3:16)? Did you contemplate the consequence of imparting erroneous ideas to your child—namely, that it would be better to have a millstone tied around your neck and cast into the depths of the sea (see Mk 9:41)?

You, as a parent, have one primary duty above all else: to prepare your child for Heaven!

You go to great lengths to care for your little one's body. You will see any doctor, spend any money, make any sacrifice to make your little one's body healthy. But faithful wisdom adds to this: think of the glorified body!

Oddly enough, when you think of earth, you may think mostly of the body, and when you think of Heaven, you may think mostly of the soul. But in a very real sense, this is backwards. As a parent, you must first consider your child's soul so that he will enjoy the glorified body in Heaven. It is counterintuitive, perhaps, but the truth is not backwards; the world is.

Reflect on your child's glorified body. To do so, consider first a beautiful diamond, as the great book *Happiness of Heaven* does so elegantly:

What is the diamond? It is nothing more than crystallized carbon, or charcoal. There is nothing in the whole range of science which can be so easily and so positively proved as this. The famous diamond Koh-i-noor, or mountain of light, which now sparkles in the British Crown . . . could, in a few moments, be reduced to a thimbleful of worthless coal dust. Yet, how great a difference, in appearance and value, between that precious gem and a thimbleful of coal dust! Again, what are other gems such as the ruby, the sapphire, the topaz, the emerald, and others? They are nothing more than crystallized clay or sand, with a trifling quantity of metallic oxide or rust, which gives to each one its peculiar color. Yet, what a difference between these sparkling and costly jewels and the shapeless clod or sand which we trample underfoot! . . .

Now if, in the natural order, God can and does transform coarse and shapeless matter into forms so beautiful and so glorious, what shall we say of the beauty and perfection into which He will change our vile bodies! For all these transformations which we now witness belong to the natural order, and are the result of the laws which govern matter in this world of imperfection; whereas our transformation in the resurrection depends on the immediate act of God's almighty power. The difference, therefore, between our present corruptible body and the

glorified body will be greater by far than the difference
we now see between charcoal and the diamond.[12]

What if you devoted all your efforts to magnifying your
child's earthly body? Specifically, you might purchase only
healthy food, turn off the TV, push your child to excel in
athletics, and take them to the best doctors. But nurturing
this little soul *now* will result in an even greater body *later*.
"Although all the just must rise in glory and in the perfection of human nature, you must not, therefore, infer that
all shall rise in the same degree of beauty and splendor of
form. For, as the resurrection is a reward to the just, it fol-
lows that each one shall have a body glorified in proportion
to his own individual merits."[13]

If your child is barely saved from hell, his or her glorified
body will be far less glorious, less able to enjoy the pleasures
of Paradise, than someone who led a devout and pious life.
You, Dad and Mom, should spend far greater effort tend-
ing to your little one's future glorified body than his temporal body, which is nothing but black coal compared to
the diamond that awaits the soul.

In *Happiness of Heaven*, Father Boudreau shows that the
corporeal attributes of Heaven are nearly opposite of our

---

[12]   J. Boudreau, *Happiness of Heaven: The Joys and Rewards of Eternal
       Glory* (Rockford, IL: TAN Books, 1984), p. 63–65.
[13]   Ibid., p. 72.

earthly experiences. The following is refreshing for those struggling through our material-obsessed world:

> It will no longer be as it is in this world, where personal beauty is a free gift of God, but no reward. Hence we see personal beauty in pagans and infidels,[14] as well as in Christians. Its possession does not, in the least, denote sanctity; nor does its absence denote moral depravity; and, therefore, beautiful persons may be very wicked, while deformed ones may be very holy. *Not so after the resurrection.* Perfect personal beauty accompanied by a heavenly splendor, being one of the rewards in store for children of God, will then denote sanctity in the just. *The more holy they have been in this life, the more beautiful and conformable to the glorious body of Jesus they shall be.*[15]

It is truly amazing when you stop and consider the following: the little body you care for so much now will, in Heaven, be as beautiful as the soul is now on earth. How often we have things backwards. *Lord forgive us Parents, for we too often obsess over the earthly body rather than the glorified body.*

---

[14]   And I might add the new pagans of our day: celebrity athletes, musicians, politicians, and every other group of persons focused on earthly appeal and success.

[15]   Ibid., pp. 72–73; emphasis added.

Father Boudreau concludes his chapter with these striking words. As he speaks to you about your own body, imagine he is speaking to you about your son or daughter's body:

Now, Christian reader, do you wish to possess faultless personal beauty in your heavenly home? Do you desire, not only to increase your own blessedness, but to be an ornament in the kingdom of your Father? No doubt you do. Well, you have the means in your hands. Lead a holy life, and a life of purity and perfect charity. Endeavor to reproduce in yourself the virtues which Jesus taught and practiced; and when the angel's trumpet calls the dead to life, your body, which must first be sown in dishonor, shall rise in that degree of beauty which you have deserved by the holiness of your life.[16]

---

[16] Ibid., pp. 73–74.

The Prodigal Son

THE VIRTUE OF PIETY

Visualization is a powerful tool. Whether an athlete envisions the shot he is about to take or the entrepreneur pictures his business in a future state, visualization of a desired outcome hones the mind in a way that no external stimulus can. Therefore, Loving Parent, visualize your child as a young man or woman before Almighty God. And what do you see? You want to see a pious man or woman, do you not?

How does piety look? What are its features? The first image that likely floods your mind is one of hands folded, eyes closed, and head bowed. Perhaps you see your son or daughter kneeling before God—or perhaps laying prostrate. Perhaps you see him or her embracing Our Lord, like the prodigal son embraced his father upon his return home. Such images come to mind when we consider piety.

And while such images are beautiful, they are incomplete in regard to the great virtue of piety. Piety comes from the Latin word *pietas* (noun), and pious from *pius* (adjective).

To the ancient Romans, *pius* was a very masculine, strong word meaning "devout" or "dutiful"—the sort of devotion a soldier held for his commander. A soldier was *pius* if he was willing to step into the breach, to hold his ground, to stare the enemy in the face, and to die for a cause greater than himself. A man's virtue was largely due to the *pietas* he held for the gods of his city. In fact, the poet Virgil used *pius* as Aeneas's common epithet in the *Aeneid*. And Christian chivalry continued the tradition in what became known as *knightly piety*—the virtue of those select men who were warriors for Christ and king.

And now we return to visualizing your son or daughter piously presenting him or herself before the throne of God. Perhaps now you see a different image. Perhaps now you see a physical strength in his or her demeanor, like a soldier standing at attention before his king, or perhaps genuflecting but leaning against his sword.

You, Dear Parent, are raising a warrior for Christ. Piety is the virtue of this warrior. Of course, the head is bowed in reverence to the King, but a firm grip holds the sword; the knee may be bent, but it is ready to spring into action to slay the demonic enemies of the kingdom.

Piety is devotion, yes, but it is passionate, strong, zealous devotion with a sense of honor and duty, never ashamed of one's faith, always ready to defend the honor of Our Lord and of Holy Mother Church.

Visualize your child in this manner, and he will be far more likely to develop the virtue of piety, which will manifest itself in every area of life. We will now examine three areas that are particularly related to the virtue of piety: the devotional life, the liturgical life, and the sacramental life.

The Devotional Life

It is an understandable though grave mistake to merely think in terms of your child practicing devotion. No! Your child's life must not merely consist of this and that devotion. Rather, your child must live the devout life. A devotion is a prayer, but St. Paul instructs you to "pray without ceasing" (1 Thes 5:17) precisely because your entire life should be a prayer. In other words, your child's life should *be* a devotion.

Your child must understand that the sole purpose of this short life is to know, love, and serve Almighty God. There is no other reason. Your child's brain was made not just to learn algebra but to know God, even if through mathematical truths. Your child's heart is not just for loving his spouse but for loving God through whatever vocation God asks him to fulfill. Your child's feet are not just for running cross-country but for walking the way of the cross. Your child's arms are not just for lifting weights but for carrying the cross of others, as Simon did for Our Lord. The purpose of your daughter's eyes is not just to glisten in beauty but to see the splendor of God in all of creation. The purpose of her mouth is not just to laugh with friends or sing but to proclaim the Word. And the purpose of every second on the twenty-four hour clock is to provide your son or daughter with one more moment of devoting him or herself to God with every ounce of possible passion. There is no other purpose in your child's life. And you, Dear Parent, must convince your child of this most sacred reality.

Your child's life is not to be lived with devotion but rather as a devotion. Prayer is not the offering to God; life is the offering—the prayer that never ceases. A prayer is merely a tool to assist in this great self-sacrifice.

Dear Parent, you must avail yourself of all the wondrous devotions Holy Mother Church offers. In order for your child's life to be truly devotional, you must help him apply the particular devotions to every area of life.

Morning Offering

When your child was young, you taught him how to go to sleep, brush his teeth, pray, and so on. But have you trained him how to arise from slumber? Have you taught your child a Morning Offering to be said directly upon waking? Is this any harder than teaching your child how to say goodnight prayers? No. You must ask yourself: why have you taught night-time prayers but not morning prayers? Perhaps the reason is that you do not make a Morning Offering upon arising, and so it is difficult to pass along what you do not have. Perhaps you put your child to bed, but he arises on his own. But maybe the real reason is that you do not see every moment of the day as devotional. Perhaps you do not see waking up as waking into the Lord's service.

From here on, teach your child how to rise like a saint. After all, it was Aristotle who famously said, "Well begun is half done." Now, when your child arises, he probably comes downstairs on his own. One of the glories of parenting is cuddling with a lethargic child in the early hours of the morning. This is the perfect time to teach him his Morning Offering. And over time, you can teach him to say it immediately upon rising.

In a little book entitled *Pray Always: A Catholic Child's First Prayer Book*,[17] you can find many simplified prayers for your son or daughter. The Morning Offering is as simple as it gets, and can thus be memorized by your little one at a very early age:

> O my God, I offer you every thought and word and act of this day. Please bless me, my God, and make me good today. Amen.

---

[17]   Conor Gallagher, *Pray Always: A Catholic Child's First Prayer Book* (Charlotte, NC: Saint Benedict Press, 2015).

And now your little one has offered his or her entire day—every thought, word, and act—to Almighty God. The devotional life for the day has begun. For this reason, the day is bound to be a holy one, and your child is bound for Heaven.

Meal Prayers

The next moment of prayer will be when your child eats breakfast. Yes, even a bowl of cereal warrants a pious folding of the hands, bowing of the head, stilling of the body, and a fervent prayer of gratitude. Do you lead by example? Certainly you do, whether it is a good or bad example. But do you rattle off *"Bless us, O Lord, and these thy gifts . . ."* as fast as possible before wolfing down your yogurt? Dear Parent, be that living catechism for your child and show them with physical reverence that you are truly grateful for the God-given nourishment.

The Angelus

And then, before dad or mom leaves for work, there is another excellent opportunity to be devout. Say the *Angelus* with your little ones.[18] Beginning the day with "*The Angel of the Lord declared unto Mary . . .*" is beautiful.

---

[18]	See the text of the Angelus in appendix 3.

Traditionally, the Angelus is prayed three times a day: 6:00 a.m., 12:00 p.m., and 6:00 p.m. As a family, you can begin the day with the Angelus, pray it before lunch, and pray it before dinner. Your child must learn that devotion is throughout the day and not just a "God bless daddy and mommy" at bedtime.

The Rosary

So many of us parents tire of the Rosary. We would rather scurry the kids to bed than struggle through another fifteen minutes with them. We prefer the XM radio station over a quiet encounter with Our Lady. We desire the blue light of Netflix rather than the blue veil of the Mother of God. If you can relate to the above, I implore you to read the following story for the sake of your child—for the Rosary is the surest means to obtaining our Blessed Mother's prayers at the hour of your child's certain death just as the young lady of the severed head came to learn:

> A certain renowned Jesuit, theologian and mystic, Father Eusebius Nierembergh tells the story that there lived in the city of Aragona, Sicily, a beautiful young lady of noble birth named Alexandra, who was courted by two young men. Out of jealousy, they one day fought, and both were killed. Their enraged relatives,

considering the young lady as the cause of this set event, murdered her, cut off her head, and threw it into a well.

Some days afterward, St. Dominic, passing by the spot and inspired by God, went to the well and cried out, "Alexandra, come forth!" In an instant the head of the murdered woman came up and remained on the edge of the well and then entreated the saint to hear her confession. The saint did so and, in the presence of an immense concourse of people, drawn there by the wonderful event, gave her communion.

He then commanded her to say for what reason she received such a great grace. Alexandra replied that when her head was cut off, she was in mortal sin but, on account of the Rosary she was in the habit of saying in her honor, the most Blessed Virgin had kept her alive. The animated head remained for two days on the edge of the well, so as to be seen by all, and thereafter the soul went to Purgatory.

A fortnight afterwards, Alexandra appeared, beautiful and shining like a star, to St. Dominic and said that the Rosary recited for the souls in Purgatory is one of the greatest reliefs that they meet in their torments and that as soon as ever they get to Heaven, they pray earnestly for those who have performed this devotion for them. Hardly had she said this when St. Dominic saw her happy soul ascend with the greatest joy to the kingdom of the Blessed.[19]

Dear Parent, perhaps your child will not be cut to pieces or thrown into a well, but he will die. And while St. Dominic may not be walking past the place of his death, hear the confession of his severed head, nor give it Communion, Our Lady will most certainly be present at his death. Be assured that if you raise your child to pray the Rosary with true devotion, the Blessed Mother will do everything in her power to bring your child to Paradise.

The Stations of the Cross

The Stations of the Cross are one of the most beautiful devotions available to us Catholics. Your child should be intimately familiar with the passion of Our Lord. This will enable him to see his own life as an ascent to Golgotha. What better way for your little one to prepare for struggle, defeat, and suffering—inevitable in this vale of tears. Nothing prevents you from praying the Stations every Friday with your little one. At the very least, it should be prayed every Friday during Lent. We will discuss later the necessity of the cross, but in terms of devotion, you must find a way to deepen your child's appreciation for Our Lord's passion.

---

[19]   Alphonsus Ligouri, *The Glories of Mary* (Charlotte, NC: TAN Books, 2012).

Holy Mother Church offers countless devotions. There are devotions to the Infant Jesus, the Precious Blood, the Holy Face, the Sacred Heart, the Divine Mercy, Our Lady of Fatima, and St. Michael, and devotions for the Holy Souls in Purgatory.[20]

Ask the Holy Spirit to guide you to the ones that are best for you and your family. More is not always better. Find your favorite novenas to your patron saint and your favorite litanies. Whatever you choose for your family, the point is to raise your child in the arms of Holy Mother Church—to live a life in which your child prays without ceasing.

The Liturgical Life

Sacred Scripture

You can tell a lot about someone by what he reads or does not read. The Bible, which was inspired by the Holy Spirit and took centuries to write and compile under the guidance of Holy Mother Church, has been sadly neglected by many parents. Rather than maintain a sacred spot in the home, the Bible is more apt to collect dust than actually be used. And as a result, our children have been under

---

[20] The book *Prayers and Heavenly Promises*, by Joan Carroll Cruz, is an outstanding little book filled with prayers and devotions to a variety of saints, to Our Lady, and to Our Lord. This book is a necessity for the pious family.

siege by Protestants and are leaving the Faith in droves for "Bible-based" churches. Reclaim, Dear Parent, our sacred patrimony. Did not St. Paul say, "Let the word of Christ dwell in you abundantly" (Col 3:16)? Put the Word of God in a place of honor in your home; read it daily with your children. Your children will either be filled with the Good News or remain empty with the world's fake news. Study Our Lord's life and meditate on His words, even more so than the words of the greatest saints. For His words are "spirit and life" (Jn 6:64), which will steer your family on the path to eternity. Above all, the best place to hear the Gospel is in the heart of the Church, in the liturgical life as it is read at Holy Mass.

Liturgical Seasons

The worldly parent focuses only on the natural seasons: fall, winter, spring, and summer. However, you, Dear Parent, child of Holy Mother Church, must not dwell solely in the natural but, more importantly, in the supernatural—that is, the Church's liturgical life. Through the liturgical seasons of Advent, Christmas, Lent, and Easter, Ordinary Time,[21] and her many feast days, the Church beckons you

---

21   The Extraordinary Form does not have Ordinary Time. Instead, the season after Epiphany, Septuagesima, and the season after Pentecost comprise the rest of the liturgical calendar.

to zealously guide your children to dive deeper into Christ's sacred mysteries. As Noah boldly summoned his family to the ark, as Joseph heroically led Mary and Jesus to Egypt, and as Sts. Louis and Zelie Martin led their children to holiness, so you too must imitate these splendid witnesses. In fact, St. Louis loved reading Dom Gueranger's *Liturgical Life* to his daughters to prepare them for the Church's great feasts. How will you prepare your little one to encounter God during the holy days and the ordinary days of his life? Will you go through the motions like our secular world, celebrating Christmas and Easter like a pagan without holy anticipation, holy sacrifice, or solemnity? Or will you allow the One who set the world into motion to redirect your child's heart to deeper conversion and gratitude for Christ's salvific work? How will you and your little one tap into the inexhaustible riches of Christ, Our Lady, St. Joseph, and the saints' feast days?

As a parent, the liturgical life must be the heart of your spiritual life because it is Christ's life made manifest in time and through the Holy Sacrifice of the Mass. The liturgical life is not some trite celebration of Christ's life; instead, the Holy Sacrifice of the Mass, the apex of the liturgical life, makes present Our Lord's sacrifice on the Cross—that is, what was, what is, and what will become before our very eyes. Hence, St. Peter Eymard, the great lover of the Holy Eucharist, once wrote about Midnight Mass, "We really go

The Flight into Egypt

to Bethlehem and we find there not a memory, not a picture, but the divine Infant Himself."[22]

Yes, Dear Parent, the liturgical life is meant to conform you and your child completely to Christ and His mysteries by the power of the Holy Spirit. It enthrones His Sacred Heart and Our Lady's Immaculate Heart in you and your little one's heart. The liturgical life is Heaven on earth; it is a foretaste of the Beatific Vision.

Our children are not conformed to Christ because we are more conformed to this fleeting world. The great apostle St. Paul declared, "Be not conformed to this world; but be reformed in the newness of your mind, that you may prove what is the good, and the acceptable, and the perfect will of God" (Rom 12:2). In each liturgical season, Dear Parent, you must lead your children to encounter Christ with renewed vigor and love.

During the Advent season, you must ready your child to meet Christ just as He will come again at the final judgment. In the Christmas season, you must prepare your child to meet Christ in His poverty and humility. In the Lenten season, you must guide your child to detach himself from this world, especially sin. Most importantly, your child must see your joy permeating through your penance and sacrifices just as Christ willingly embraced His cross.

---

[22]   Peter Julian Eymard, *The Real Presence: Eucharistic Meditations* (New York: The Sentinel Press, 1938), pp. 239–40.

During Holy Week and then in the Easter Season, you must accompany your child to the "solemnity of solemnities," the foretaste of eternity by dying with Christ in order to rise with Him. But what about the ordinary? Yes, the liturgical season of Ordonary Time composes the lengthiest season in the Church. Never tire, Dear Parent, of living the ordinary in an extraordinary way.

While the Church looks forward to her great feast days like Christmas and Easter, just as your child looks forward to his own milestones—such as obtaining his driver's license, attending college, getting married, being ordained a priest—you must show him that God is found most in the present moment, in the humble workshop of Nazareth where Our Lord spent thirty years of His life.

The Liturgical Calendar

Our secular world remembers its heroic leaders, presidents, and significant historical dates with greater affection than many of us recall our saintly brothers and sisters who have persevered in the Faith. Schools and offices are closed to honor mere men who often sought their own glory. It is time for you, Dear Parent, to remember the great exemplars of our Faith—men and women who sought only God's glory.

The greatest homage you can give to these heavenly friends is to attend Holy Mass in their honor or invoke their intercession frequently. Develop a special devotion to the saints, and teach your children to do so, especially the ones they are named after. Dear Parent, we do not always choose the saints; they often choose us. The struggles they faced and overcame are likely the same as those you and your little ones are now encountering. Never go a day without seeking their help. Make no mistake: the saints long to help us infinitely more than any of our earthly friends.

Remember this, Dear Parent, the earth's axis towards the sun causes the seasons to change; so too, Dear Parent, your liturgical devotion and piety towards the Eucharistic Son and love for the saints will cause your children's hearts to be set ablaze with fire.

The Sacramental Life

Baptism

How silly we humans can be.

Have you gone to great lengths to celebrate your child's birthday? Have you put time and energy into buying and wrapping the perfect gift? Have you bought the ingredients and baked an elaborate cake? Have you inflated the balloons and hung the streamers, invited family and friends,

The Baptism of Christ

and hosted a magnificently themed party—Star Wars . . . Dinosaurs . . . Dora the Explorer . . . Unicorns.

Silly? No. Not particularly. You love your little one. And that is a beautiful thing. But I ask you this: do you even know your child's baptismal date? You go to great lengths to celebrate the day your child left the womb, yet you do not know the date your child became a temple of the Holy Spirit. You spend hours every single year celebrating a physical birth, but *never* a spiritual birth?

Silly? Yes. Celebrating the flesh without celebrating the spirit is silly, to say the least.

And what lesson does this convey to your little one? What if you, Dear Parent, threw a modest birthday party, with modest gifts, but treated her baptismal day with splendor and rejoicing? What if you said with a big smile, "On this day, you became a beloved child of God through the waters of Holy Baptism. This is your true birthday: for you were born in the Spirit, bound for eternity in Heaven."

If you fail to celebrate the most glorious day in your child's life, the day of Baptism, you are not alone. But upon consideration, perhaps you feel foolish for celebrating the flesh more than the spirit.

Seeing the soul as the realest of realities is a continual earthly struggle, for our eyes are often affixed on the things below. It is understandable. It is, we pray, forgivable. But you, as a parent of a little soul, are called to something far greater than what worldly parents offer their children. You are called to look at your son or daughter and to see both body and soul, while giving greater importance to the latter.

Celebrate the soul. Celebrate the soul's great cleanse. Celebrate the day that the Lord adopted your child as His own. Celebrate the day your child became bound for Heaven.

The Blessings of Confession

The great little booklet entitled *Confession: Its Fruitful Practice* begins with a passage I could never replicate. It is worthy of citing in full. As you read it, consider the blessings available to your little one—and if you really desire anything greater for him in this life:

> "Blessed are they that wash their robes in the Blood of the Lamb" (Rev. 22:14). Catholics truly may be called "blessed" in the means they have of washing the sin-stained robes of their souls in the Precious Blood of the Lamb of God in the Sacrament of Penance!
>
> Man can hope for no greater blessing on this earth than true peace of soul. The Sacrament of Penance is a perennial fountain of peace. It is a source of untold consolation to human hearts.
>
> This Sacrament gives any and every member of the Catholic Church who has transgressed the holy laws of

God an easy and simple means to obtain full pardon and to be restored to His friendship. This is its first and principle effect. Its second effect is to wipe out the punishment due to sin: eternal punishment entirely, and temporal punishment in whole or in part, according to the penitent's disposition.

It closes the gates of Hell, which open to swallow up in the infernal abyss souls who deliberately turn away from God by mortal sin and who sunder the ties binding them to Him by preferring their own wills to His. A good Confession opens anew the portals of Heaven, which are barred to souls so long as they remain in the state of mortal sin.

It clothes souls with the beautiful nuptial garment of Sanctifying Grace, or renders that garment still more beautiful if the soul already possesses it.

It restores past merits, which are lost by a single mortal sin.

It renders the soul capable again of performing acts meritorious of an eternal reward, which is impossible while it is in the state of mortal sin.

It confers sacramental graces, that is, powerful supernatural helps to avoid sin in the future, and to persevere in the service of God.[23]

---

[23]   *Confession: Its Fruitful Practice with an Examination of Conscience* (Charlotte, NC: TAN Books, 2000), pp. 1–2.

Such a description of the blessings of this sacrament should excite any parent to the point of making confession a frequent occurrence for their family.

It is beyond certain that your child will face temptation in this life. It is near certain that your son or daughter will fall in big ways or small. But what is equally certain is that God awaits your repentant child in the confessional, *just as* the loving father in Christ's parable awaited his prodigal son.

The Habit of Frequent Confession

While I have no doubt in the Real Presence of the Holy Eucharist and am thus thrilled to see my young adult children in Adoration, I am overwhelmed with joy when I see them in line for confession. I do not speculate as to their sins; my only concern is their repentance.

Of all the habits you can form in your child's life—nutrition, fitness, hard work, good manners—the habit of frequent confession is perhaps the single most important of all. In fact, frequent and contrite confession *must* come before frequent Communion. Our Lord and Our Lady are offended by the vast numbers of unworthy communicants. It is a sacrilege to receive the True Presence into your flesh when a sin of grave matter is upon your soul. Thus, training your little one in frequent confession increases the likelihood of a worthy Eucharistic reception.

Your weekly family schedule fills up quickly. Every Monday and Wednesday is soccer practice; every Thursday is mom's night out; every Saturday is date night. But where is confession? Imagine if your family rotated its week around becoming Heaven bound.

When you, Dear Parent, are nothing but rotting flesh and decaying bones, will your fifty-year-old daughter still be driving to soccer practice? No! But will she have the chance to drive herself and, pray God, her own children to confession? Yes. So long as your child is living in the civilized world, she will have this glorious option. Form the habit in your little one now.

The Adult Child's Return to the Sacraments

And here is a difficult reality for many parents to swallow—and I say it with sympathy and charity: the greatest sorrow you should feel as a parent is not whether your grown child is unemployed or divorced or even deathly ill. Rather, it is when your grown child freely chooses to abandon the sacrament of confession.

How many faithful parents experience the absolute heartache of their adult children leaving the Church—usually after they send them to a secular university? And those loving parents repeatedly invite their sons and daughters to Holy

Mass, desperately wanting their children to come back into the fold.

But do not make the grievous mistake of equating Holy Mass with receiving Holy Communion.

One of the reasons the grown child no longer desires Holy Communion is because he stopped going to confession. And to admit someone to Holy Communion without proper contrition and reception of absolution is a sacrilege. From the vantage point of the adult child, it is also a cheapening of the Eucharist into something he can get whenever he chooses rather than understanding the Eucharist as a privilege he no longer deserves. If he can just—on a whim—come back to Communion, there is nothing special about it.

No! The loving parent who wants his child to return to Holy Mass *must* tell him frankly, "Yes, please come to Mass with the family. Sit with us. Pray with us. You are not only welcome but greatly desired. But, my son or daughter, you must go to confession before receiving Holy Communion. I will move mountains to help you with this. But if you have any grave matter on your soul, the *worst thing* you can do is receive Holy Communion. I love both Our Lord and you too much to encourage you in any other way." This, Dear Parent, is the truth. But anything else is both a sacrilege and a cheapening of the sacrament in the eyes of your beloved child. Explaining the necessity for confession is the surest way for your child, young or old, to regain appreciation for the Holy Eucharist.

Satan and the Sacrament of Confession

In the jarring little book *Triumph of the Blessed Sacrament over Beelzebub*, the prolific author Father Michael Mueller recounts the incredible story of a young French lady named Nicola Aubry who was possessed by demons in 1563. Her exorcism lasted several months. In those days, priests would often perform the Rite of Exorcism in church, in full view of the public. Many witnesses confirmed the remarkable events of this exorcism and many incredible stories are available to anyone who desires to see the Holy Eucharist's triumph over the devil. One such story shows the power of confession over the devil himself:

> One day, during one of the exorcisms in church, the evil spirit was chattering and uttering all kinds of nonsense. Suddenly he stopped short and gazed fixedly at a young man who was eagerly forcing his way through the crowd, in order to have a nearer view of the possessed woman. The devil saluted him in a mocking tone. "Good-morning, Peter!" said he. "Come here and take a good view of me. Ah, Peter! I know that you are a freethinker, but tell me where were you last night?" And then the devil related, in the presence of everyone

in church, a shameful sin that Peter had committed the preceding night. He described all the circumstances with such precision, that Peter was overwhelmed with confusion, and could not utter a word. "Yes," cried the devil, in a mocking tone, "you have done it; you dare not deny it."

Peter hurried away as fast as he could, muttering to himself, "The devil tells the truth; I thought that no one knew it but myself, and God."

Peter seemed to have forgotten that the devil is the witness of our evil actions, that he remembers them all well, and that, at the hour of death, he will bring them all against us, as he himself declared.

"For it is thus," he added in a rage, "that I take revenge on sinners." Peter had not been to Confession for many years, and, as a natural consequence, his morals were not exactly of the purest order. He had been guilty of what the fashionable world calls "*pardonable weaknesses*," "*slight indiscretions*," etc. The public accusation of the devil filled him with wholesome confusion. He rushed into the confessional, cast himself at the feet of a priest, and received absolution. After having finished his Confession, Peter had the boldness to press through the crowd once more; but this time he kept at a respectful distance from his infernal accuser. The exorcist saw Peter, and knowing that he had been at Confession, he told him to draw near. Then pointing to him, the exorcist said to the devil, "See here, do you know this man?"

The devil raised his eyes and leisurely surveyed Peter from head to foot, and from right to left. At last he said, "Why! really, it *is* Peter."

"Well!" said the exorcist, "do you know anything else about him?"

"No," answered the devil, "nothing else."

The devil had no longer any knowledge of Peter's sins, because they had been entirely blotted out by the Blood of Jesus Christ, in the holy Sacrament of Confession. What the priest forgives on earth, God forgives in Heaven.

As a parent, you must teach your child that the devil is alive and prowling about the world, seeking the ruin of souls (1 Pt 5:8). But nothing destroys the devil's knowledge over his prey more than the power of absolution. The devil has no power against the blood of Jesus Christ, which washes away our sins.

The Holy Eucharist

Let us now turn to the greatest subject in all the world, in all the cosmos; let us turn to the subject that causes every angel to bend his knee and bow his head, while causing every demon to vomit in disgust, to snarl in fury, to shriek in agony: that is none other than the Blessed Eucharist.

Belief in the True Presence

Consider, Dear Parent, what if news pinged and dinged through every social media outlet and news channel that Jesus Christ had appeared in your parish? Flocks of people—believers and non-believers alike—would flood the sanctuary, crowd the streets, and fling themselves prostrate before Our Lord's flesh and blood.

Would you load up your child immediately into the car? Would you skip soccer practice? Would you postpone your chores? Would you and your spouse look at each other with wonder and awe and with a bit of fear and trepidation? Would your heart pound? Would your mind race with memories of shame and remorse? And how would you prepare your child for this miracle? What words would you use to inspire him, to focus his mind? Might you worry that the end of the world was upon you, your spouse, and your little one?

And upon standing before Jesus Christ in the flesh, how would you conduct yourself? Would you be overly worried about the state of your hair or your newest outfit, or perhaps a bit more concerned with the state of your soul? Would you be directing and even begging your children of all ages to gaze upon their God with the most profound reverence? And seeing their inability to do so, would you regret missing the countless opportunities to teach them how? And how ashamed might you feel if your teenagers checked their smartphones before He who died on the cross for them? And how ashamed might you be if Jesus asks you and your spouse, "Why do you act so piously now?" You reply, "You are my Lord, my Savior." He then asks you and your spouse, "But why are you acting differently than ever before?" You answer, "Because I have never seen You before." He slowly shakes His head and says the very words he said two thousand years ago, "Blessed are they that have not seen, and have believed" (Jn 20:29).

Perhaps this image helps us see what little faith we possess. But not all of us. The elect, those few who enter through the narrow way (see Mt 7:14) do not need eyes to see the flesh and blood of Jesus Christ. *And neither must your children!*

A great French king and saint of the Church, Louis IX, did not need his eyes to believe. Father Michael Mueller, one of the greatest lovers of the Eucharist, tells the following story in his masterpiece *The Blessed Eucharist: Our Greatest Treasure*:[24] "One day, when St. Louis, King of France, was

---

[24]   In the humble opinion and limited experience of the author, this is one of the greatest works on the Holy Eucharist ever written. This is a masterpiece that sings out to the soul the glories of our

invited to go to a church in which Our Lord appeared in the Holy Eucharist under the form of an infant, he replied: 'I will not go to see my Lord in the Holy Eucharist because I believe that He is present there as firmly as if I had seen Him. Let those go and see Him who do not believe.'"[25]

And so, Good Parent, I ask again: what would you do if Our Lord appeared in flesh and blood in your parish? A saint would answer, "Nothing different than I do every Sunday." But are we not all sinners? While we should marvel at the miraculous occurrences, they are only performed for the sake of emboldening our faith. Believe without seeking miracles! Believe with the eyes of faith, not because science fails to explain away Eucharistic miracles. Believe, even though the appearance of bread and wine stares back at you.

Let us consider why Our Eucharistic Lord hides Himself from you and your family. If Jesus wants your little first communicant in her pretty dress and veil to believe in Him, why does He not show Himself? If you ask this, you have asked an excellent question.

Greatest Treasure, that pleads with us to treat the Eucharist just as we would God himself, for it truly is God! Read this book and your life will never be the same. Read this book and you will see that raising your kids with a love of the Eucharist is your greatest calling as a parent.

[25] Michael Mueller, *Blessed Eucharist: Our Greatest Treasure* (Charlotte, NC: TAN Books, 2010), p. 11.

In *The Blessed Eucharist*, Father Mueller explains two reasons why Our Lord hides Himself in the Eucharist:

> But you perhaps ask: "Why does Our Lord hide Himself under the outward appearance of bread and wine? Why does He not manifest Himself under the sensible qualities of His Body, with His wounded hands, His merciful countenance, His radiant majesty?" Now, Our Lord does so chiefly for two reasons: The first is that we may not lose the merit of faith. Were we to see Jesus Christ as He is seen by the blessed in Heaven, we could no longer make an act of faith in His Real Presence, for "faith is the belief in things we do not see." (St. Paul)
>
> Now Our Lord wishes to bestow on us after this life a great reward for our faith, as He Himself has said: "Blessed are they that do not see and yet believe." Many of the Saints, in order not to lose the merit of their faith, have gone so far as to beg Our Lord not to favor them those consoling manifestations of Himself in the Blessed Sacrament which He has sometimes granted to His chosen servants. . . .
>
> The second reason why Our Lord hides Himself is that He might inspire us with confidence. If He were to show Himself in all His glory, as He appears to the Angels and Saints in Heaven, who would dare to approach Him? Surely no one. But Jesus most earnestly desires to unite Himself intimately to our souls, and therefore He conceals Himself under the outward form of bread, that

we may not be afraid of Him. "Our great King," says St. Teresa, "veils Himself that we may receive Him with greater confidence."

Help your child understand these two reasons: first, because your little one must see the Eucharist with the eyes of faith, for our eternal reward is largely based upon this very faith. Imagine the standard to which your child would be held if he had the Beatific Vision on earth! In this manner, we ought to thank God for withholding Himself from our eyes during this earthly life. And secondly, God hides Himself from your little one so that your child can approach the altar rail with confidence. Your child could not endure seeing Our Lord in His triumphant glory. But Jesus Christ comes to your child under the appearance of a little wafer and a little wine—something so small and innocent. How precious that your first communicant, at the mere age of seven, can receive the God of the universe into his little body and God's sanctifying grace into his little soul.

Reverence for the Blessed Eucharist

As the primary educators, you must teach your child Eucharistic piety above all else. Show him your lively example and vibrant faith in the Eucharist. Show him that your faith is so strong that your body changes in His presence. The mighty father who—to a little one—is the strongest man in the world meekly genuflects before the tabernacle and prostrates before the exposed Presence in the monstrance. Mighty father of the little one: show your weakness, your frailty, your total and complete subjection to the King of the Universe. Let your little one marvel at your physical demeanor, for nowhere else in life will the little one see Daddy so meek, with eyes cast down and head bowed and knees bent and hands folded and heart overwhelmed with humility. Show your son, who will one day be a man like you, that you know nothing, you possess nothing, and you are nothing before the Blessed Eucharist.

And Mommy: surrender all your candor and competence, all your order and structure, all your delicacy and decorum, all your feminine savvy and strength to the True Presence. Offer every ounce of your body and soul, every ounce of your purity, every ounce of your beauty. Allow your son to see the true beauty of a woman completely subordinate to the King of kings; allow your daughter to see what a real woman does at her most productive and fruitful time.

Your children will learn more from your physical de-meanor before the True Presence than they will learn in all the manners you instill, in all the homework they do, and from all the catechesis you teach them.

Hear me, Dear Parent: your *body* is the truest catechism for your little ones before the Blessed Eucharist.

Visiting the Blessed Sacrament

Have you considered the indescribable fortune of having the Blessed Eucharist down the street from your son or daughter? How far would you take your little one to receive and be received by Our Lord? And might you, after reading the little passage below, forever explain the story of the Magi differently to your little ones?

"Where is the newborn King of the Jews?" inquired the three Magi of Herod, king of Jerusalem. "Where is He?" they repeat in their great desire to find Him. . . . Beloved Christian, you have heard and read this incident among the many wonderful events in the life of our God and Saviour. On hearing or reading the account, you have perhaps even earnestly desired to have lived at the times of the Apostles in order that you might have had the happiness of seeing your Lord and Saviour. But you ought to know that you are happier now than if you had lived at that time of the Apostles, for you might have been obliged to travel very far and make many inquiries to find out the place of His abode. But now there is no need of traveling far or of making many inquiries to find Him. He is, as we know by faith, in our churches, not far from our homes. The Magi could find Him in one place only; we can find Him in every part of the world, wherever the Blessed Sacrament is kept.[26]

---

[26] Michael Mueller, *Blessed Eucharist*, p. 48.

How many quick stops you make at the grocery store! How easily you pick up a coffee in the drive-through! How much enjoyment you get out of grabbing a quick lunch with your friend! But the best you get is a filled belly, a caffeine fix, or a few laughs.

All the while, Our Lord waits alone in the tabernacle, awaiting you. He offers heavenly nourishment that will never leave one hungry; He offers an inexhaustible source of vigor and zeal and passion, not mere spurts of energy that burn out with the setting sun; He offers an all-loving ear to hear your worries, an omnipotent shoulder to cry upon, an everlasting friendship that will never let you down. And He has made Himself available in every Catholic church on earth. He awaits you. Like His apostles in the garden, He beseeches us, "Could you not spend time with me?" (see Mt 6:40). Or like the Father said to Adam and Eve after sinning, "Where are you?" (see Gn 3:9). Perhaps more importantly, He asks you, "Where are your little ones?" Did He not say that you must let the little children come unto Him (see Mk 10:14; Mt 19:14)?

How steadfast you are, Dear Parent, in taking your child to the doctor, to the dentist, to the ophthalmologist, anyone and everyone needed to care for that little body. But please consider that the little body will turn to dust, the teeth will decay, the eyes will lose their sight. Yet that little soul—made in the image and likeness of Almighty

God—will forever remain, long past when the earth can sustain life, long past when the sun burns out. Tonight, go outside with your little one, look up at the night sky; explain to your child how ancient the stars are and how it has taken millions of years for the light to reach our planet; explain how those billions and billions of stars will continue to dazzle the universe for billions and billions of years, long after our planet loses all its beautiful color of green life and blue water. And then look at your child and say, "But you, dear little one, will outlive every star in the sky. Your soul will burn bright after every one of those specks in the heavens have vanished into nothingness. You are immortal. You will see Mars turn to dust. You will see the greatest stars become tiny pebbles floating in space. You will outlive every material object in God's vast universe. Why? Because God loves you more than every comet, more than every planet and every black hole and every star. God made you in His image and likeness so that you can be with Him forever and ever and ever."

Have you, Loving Parent, considered that your child's soul will outlive everything in the material universe? Consider this next time you tell her to brush her decaying teeth but fail to help her examine her immortal conscience. Consider this next time you scurry her around town in the minivan to this or that doctor but fail to visit the Divine Physician awaiting in the Blessed Eucharist in the golden tabernacle just miles away from where you are sitting at this very moment.

Take your little one—for five minutes! What? You have no time? You have too much to do? Too many errands to run? Our Eucharistic Lord knows that children can't sit still; He made them that way. He knows that children don't understand the sacramental mysteries; He will reveal the truths in His own time. He knows that you, Father and Mother, are exhausted and just want to get "stuff" done, but He calls you, as parent, to so much more than efficiency. Your child does not need to be an honor student or a great athlete or musician. But your son or daughter *needs* to learn that the Blessed Eucharist is the answer to all of life's problems.

In *The Blessed Eucharist*, Father Mueller challenges the reader to consider life's problems in light of the blessings available to us. As a parent, all of your attention and energy should go in to helping your child, regardless of age, understand the following:

> Why should you take life so hard and complain of your crosses and trials and be so impatient in every difficulty? Why should you envy the rich of this world, the great and the honored? Why should you vex yourself at injuries and groan in adversity? Why should you faint at the thought of self-denial and conflict? *Are you not a Catholic?* Have you not the sweet services of the Church

to soothe you and her Sacraments to nourish you, her benedictions to strengthen you and her absolution to cleanse you? Have you not Mary for your Mother and the Angels and Saints for your patrons and protectors, and above all, in the Blessed Sacrament, Jesus for your Father?[27]

Do you teach your child that the Blessed Sacrament is the fulfillment of his desires and the solution to his struggles? Do you realize it for yourself? How foolish we can be, seeking worldly answers to everything.

You, my Dear Parent, are Catholic! You are Catholic! This means that you have, as Father Mueller explained so elegantly, unimaginable access to grace through the Church, the sacraments, and most especially, the Blessed Sacrament.

Take your children to the Divine Physician. Take them soon. If this little book has stirred up the slightest feeling of zeal, take them very soon, even if you must sit outside in the parking lot. Let your child know that God is truly present in the Eucharist just on the other side of the wall. And then pray, Father and Mother, that for the rest of your child's life that he will turn to the Eucharist in times of joy and in times of sorrow. If this happens with your influence, you, Dear Parent, will have done your job. And Jesus Christ, the Second Person of the Blessed Trinity, will say to

---

[27]   Michael Mueller, *Blessed Eucharist*, p. 91; emphasis added.

you, "Well done, good and faithful servant" (Mt 25:23). Just imagine. . .

Holy Matrimony

You pray for your child. You help him pray his innocent little prayers at bedtime. You desire for him to grow into a healthy, happy adult—fulfilled, dignified, respected, accomplished. And all this is beautiful.

But how often we forget the other half of your child. What could I possibly mean? I mean your son's future wife and your daughter's future husband—if God so wills.

Look upon your little one. If you can, look at him right now. Is he playing in the back yard on the swings? Coloring a picture? Is he peacefully napping? Or perhaps he is no longer so little. Is he driving to school or work? Is he in college right now?

See what your little one (who may not be so little) is doing at this particular stage in life. Now, comprehend that his future wife is most likely doing something very similar at this moment, for they are probably close in age. If your son is crawling, there is a good chance his future wife is crawling. If he is starting to notice young women, then she is starting to notice young men.

In other words, your child's future spouse is not an idea. No! He or she is a flesh and blood person. Your daughter's future husband is now forming good and bad habits and opening himself up and closing himself off to God's grace. He desperately needs your prayers as much as your own daughter does.

Consider, Dear Parent: how much of your own happiness or sadness comes from your marriage? How important to your own well-being and to your children's well-being are the virtues and vices of your spouse? Is your wife overly critical? Does your husband suffer from anger? Is your wife subject to the sins of gossip and pride? Is your husband a slave to lust? On the other hand, is your husband a strong and faithful husband? Is your wife a tender and loving wife? So much of our joy and so much of our sorrow comes from our other self, for the two become one flesh (see Mk 10:8–10).

Imagine that God revealed to you the little boy that your little girl will one day marry. And this little boy lives next door. You see the trials and tribulations of this little boy, for his parents are imperfect. You see how his good looks and intelligence become sources of vanity. You see that his courage often becomes rashness and foolishness. You see all the normal processes that a young man goes through as he finds his way into manhood. But if you could help this little boy in his time of need, if you could help shape his character, if you could aid him to avoid extremes, if you could somehow get him to confession and Holy Mass more frequently, if you could do all these things and more to help prepare a most worthy husband for your daughter, would you not do so?

Of course you would. You would surely give as much attention to this child as you do your own, for your own child's happiness in this life is largely dependent on the virtue of his or her future spouse.

Dear Parent, hear me: you can, right now, pray for that little boy or little girl. Commit yourself, right now, to praying for your future son-in-law and daughter-in-law every single day that you remain on this earth.

As you pray for your children, one by one, now add their future spouses, for they are not an idea; they are living and breathing and desperately need your prayers.

And furthermore, tonight, when you tuck your little one into bed, begin the practice of praying for his future spouse *with him!* He will look at you funny. He may even laugh. But over time, he will begin to understand something so powerful that it will change his life forever. He will be keenly aware that his future wife is out there in the world and needs prayers.

Yes, your ten-year-old daughter can understand that *if* God calls her to Holy Matrimony, she can begin the beautiful spousal task of praying for her spouse. Imagine, Loving Parent, that your daughter has been praying for this young man every night for three years. And now she is sixteen, and boys are interested in her. But every single night, she has been praying for that one special young man. She already loves him, though she knows not exactly who he is. Thus, she sees the silly boys flirting with her for nothing more than that. And she awaits her husband in purity and anticipation. And now she is twenty-two, graduating college. She has passed up many temptations. She has turned away many interested boys. For twelve years, every single night—which is 4,380 nights—she has prayed for this young man. She has gone into Adoration countless times throughout college, gazed upon Jesus Christ in the Eucharist, and smiled as her heart turned towards her future husband, who was once a boy in her mind and is now a man, roaming the world in search of her. In a sense, she knows him. And in fact, she loves him. She awaits him to find her. She is ready for him. And she turns her heart back to the Blessed Eucharist and says with sincerest love, "Bring him to me, Lord. But care for him, O Lord, until I can."

And now, Dad and Mom, imagine she has found him. Finally, the young man drops to one knee and proposes. She can look down upon him with that same loving gaze that gazed upon Our Lord in Adoration; she looks at him with those same eyes that tightly closed when she was a uttering the little prayers at ten years old; she can look down upon him and say, "I have been with you every day since I was ten years old. I have held you in my mind and in my heart. You have been on my lips thousands of times as I offered you to God's care. I love you, but I have always loved you. And I answer *yes*, I will be your wife, but in a sense, I have always belonged to you, and you to me. You are not just the man of my marriage, but the man of my life, for my father and mother gave you to me as a little girl in my night-time prayers. You are the man of my life, and so I accept your proposal with all my heart."

Holy Orders

The sacredness of the priesthood should be a penetrating reality for your child. Such unworthy men, becoming *in persona Christi*, the sacramentally conferred power consecrating the bread and wine into the Body and Blood of Jesus Christ and to forgive sins on behalf of Christ; it is beyond what the mind can fathom.

And while not deemed to be Holy Orders, religious life is astoundingly beautiful, particularly in the barbaric age in which we live. Nothing is more beautiful than to see a young woman forgo the pleasures of the world, the natural longings for a husband and child, and to see her don the veil of a bride to Christ.

Most likely, you know plenty of priests. Whether you like them or not, it is paramount to kindle within your child's heart a grave respect for the offices of the deacon, the priest,

The Last Supper

and the bishop. And if the man is a scandal—as so many are—focus on the glories of the office, on the apostolic succession, and on the preservation of the ecclesial ranks by the Holy Spirit throughout the ages.

It is less likely, however, that you have good religious sisters in your area. If you do, count your blessings. Seeing a faithful nun in full habit is, to your little one, a small touch of Heaven. There is something mystical about a woman in a habit, for it is a physical proclamation of her total rejection of the world and total submission to Jesus Christ.

Loving Parent, go out of your way to show your child such women. It goes without saying that religious garb does not make the man or woman. But it should likewise go without saying that a lapel pin is not inspiring to a little girl or boy.

Regarding vocational discernment, instruct your child from the earliest age—and progressively so as the years pass—that it is every young man and woman's moral duty to discern a religious calling. And a passing thought is utterly insufficient. No, your child must persistently pray over the matter. Look for vocational retreats. Introduce your son to various religious orders and various holy priests in your diocese. In fact, add it into the typical college search.

Always emphasize that you are not imposing a religious vocation on them. But likewise emphasize that it is your solemn duty to help your child discover God's calling for his or her life.

Your child is more likely to be called to Holy Matrimony than religious life or Holy Orders. Nonetheless, parents make the grave mistake of not giving such vocations ample time to reach fruition in the heart and mind of their child. Never let a day pass without praying a Hail Mary for your child's future vocation, for the grace that he or she might know and generously follow the path God has destined for all eternity.[28]

---

[28]   See A Prayer for Your Child's Vocation in appendix 4.

THE VIRTUE OF HUMILITY

"In Paradise there are many Saints who never gave alms on earth: their poverty justified them. There are many Saints who never mortified their bodies by fasting or wearing hair shirts: their bodily infirmities excused them. There are many Saints too who were not virgins: their vocation was otherwise. But in Paradise there is no Saint who was not humble."[29]

This is the opening paragraph to the greatest book I have ever read: *Humility of Heart* by Father Cajetan Mary da Bergamo (1672–1753). If you read but one book outside Holy Scripture, if you can convince your grown child to read but one book in his or her life, I recommend it be this one amidst the tens of thousands of great Catholic works penned over two thousand years.

How can one make such a claim? Because, truly, humility is the root of all virtue and pride is the root of all sin.

---

[29]   Cajetan Mary da Bergamo, *Humility of Heart* (Charlotte, NC: TAN Books, 2011), p. 1.

Without humility, you cannot be devoted to Our Lord; you cannot be a loving spouse or loving parent; you cannot be a true friend. You, Christian Reader, are *nothing* without the virtue of humility.

What will God call your little girl to be? A mother of ten? An astronaut? A scientist that cures cancer? A cloistered nun? You do not know.

And what will He call your little son to be? A Navy SEAL? A small business entrepreneur? A professor? A parish priest? You do not know.

But you do know with absolute certainty that the Second Person of the Blessed Trinity is directly calling your son or daughter to "learn of me, because I am meek, and humble of heart" (Mt 11:29). Father Cajetan explains:

> He has not called everyone to be doctors, preachers or priests, nor has He bestowed on all the gift of restoring sight to the blind, healing the sick, raising the dead or casting out devils, but to all He has said: "Learn of Me, to be humble of heart," and to all He has given the power to learn humility of Him. . . . The Savior might have said: "Learn of Me to be chaste, humble, prudent, just, wise, abstemious, etc." But He only says: "Learn of Me, because I am meek and humble of heart." (Matt. 11:29). And in humility alone He includes all things, because as St. Thomas so truly says, "Acquired humility is in a certain sense the greatest good." Therefore who-

ever possesses this virtue may be said, as to his proxi-
mate disposition, to possess all virtues, and he who lacks
it, lacks all.[30]

Dear Parent, you walk a fine line—seemingly—between
teaching your child humility and developing a strong
self-esteem. The world has never, nor ever will, esteem humility. Just look around: everything is geared towards vanity, self-promotion, and self-indulgence. Truly, your child is
growing up in unprecedented times of vanity.

What is important to understand, however, is that true
self-esteem comes from humility. Humility is, rather simply
put, the proper knowledge of self in relation to God. How
on earth could you not want your child to know where he
stands in relation to God?

Scripture repeatedly says that you are nothing before
God. In fact, the trial of Job was all about him learning
to not even question God but to humbly accept whatever
God sent his way.

There is nothing more freeing for your child than to
know that Almighty God is infinitely greater, more powerful, more knowledgeable than he ever will be. This does
not destroy the child's confidence. No! It gives him a
greater sense of security, of purpose, and of placement in
the universe.

---

[30]　Ibid., pp. 2–3.

And so, as a parent, you must raise your child to see all things from the standpoint of pride and humility. True, your child naturally gravitates towards certain vices: gluttony, anger, sloth . . . But you must creatively and insightfully show your son or daughter that these sins are rooted in pride. If your daughter struggles with gluttony, it is because she believes she has the right to indulge to make herself feel better rather than humbly turning to God in her distress! If your son struggles with anger, it is because he feels himself superior to those who cross him rather than humbly and patiently enduring the injustice. No matter the sin, identify and articulate the prideful root of that particular vice. Train your child's mind to detect the presence of pride.

In like manner, when you witness virtue in your child's life or the life of others, intentionally point out the beauty of humility present therein. For example, if your middle schooler offers the front seat to a younger sibling, instead of saying, "That was kind of you," consider saying, "That was kind *and* humble of you." You might get a double look; it will catch your child off guard. He was not trying, *per se*, to be humble, but kind. If your teenager agrees to set aside the smart phone, instead of saying, "Proud of you! That takes self-discipline," try saying, "Proud of you! That takes discipline *and* a hefty dose of humility." It is your responsibility to teach your children, of all ages, that humility is the foundation of their good behavior. They must learn to see the spiritual life through the lens of pride and humility.

Humility is everything. And a saint learns how to view all thoughts, words, and actions as either acts of pride or acts of humility, for truly, every thought, word, and action is taking us closer to God or further from Him.

Towards God

Your duty as a parent is to teach your child to render himself entirely obedient to God. Period. There is no consolation prize for the parent who neglects this one divinely given duty. If your child is elected president of the United States or appointed to the Supreme Court but is not humble before God, he or she has amounted to nothing. Ask yourself: would you be "proud" if your child cured cancer but took the credit rather than giving it to God?

Remember this: the world does not value humility. But will you?

Teaching your child that his successes come from God is paramount in the spiritual life. "The truly humble man considers that whatever is good in his material or spiritual nature is like unto the streams that have come originally from the sea and must eventually return to the sea, and therefore he is always careful to render to God all that he has received from God, and neither prays for nor loves nor

Christ Crucified

desires anything except that all things the name of God be sanctified: 'Hallowed be Thy name' (Matt. 6:9)."[31]

When your child succeeds in small ways or great, tell him immediately to thank God for his blessings. Eliminate the word *luck* from his vocabulary; help him learn that all things are the result of divine providence. "We were lucky to have good weather during the game" must become "We were blessed to have good weather during the game."

Gaze at the stars with your little one and explain the vastness of the universe. Tell your child that there are an estimated two hundred billion galaxies. Tell your little one that holding a grain of sand up against the sky covers up ten thousand galaxies. Tell your son that God holds each one in the palm of His hand. Tell him that humility is understanding God's magnificent power, and that before Him we are nothing—like a speck of sand in the vast universe. But then emphasize that despite our smallness and insignificance, God became flesh and dwelt among us. And as the ultimate sign of His humility, He allowed the Roman soldiers to put Him to death.

Hope and pray, Loving Parent, that your child will mature with a keen sense of wonder and awe at God's majesty and the fragility of life, particularly his own mind, power, and goodness. By marveling at the Infinite, you will give your child a sense of joy and gratitude, and, yes, a sense

---

[31]   Ibid., p. 38.

THE VIRTUE OF HUMILITY   81

of self-worth, for every fiber of his worth comes directly from God.

Indeed, the greatest commandment is an act of humility, bowing before His majesty. "And thou shalt love the Lord thy God, with thy whole heart, and with thy whole soul, and with thy whole mind, and with thy whole strength" (Mk 12:30).

Towards Others

"And the second is like to it: Thou shalt love thy neighbour as thyself" (Mk 12:31).

What a perfect expression of humility towards others. Truly, it is a great act of humility to love another person, especially those who irritate you.

Your neighbor may be your superior, your equal, or your subordinate. But how do you treat each of these? How do you teach your child to respect each of these? Oh, how often, Dear Parent, have you seen your child compare himself to others! How often have you heard your teenager make a subtle but prideful remark about how the awkward kid looks, walks, acts, or sounds! How often have you heard your child return one verbal blow for another! If you desire humility yourself, then you must be reminded that your child has learned more about pride from you than anyone else.

So how must the truly humble man act towards others? *Humility of Heart* lays out the cold, hard truth—a truth ever so difficult to internalize:

> The truly humble man believes that everyone is better than himself, and that he is the worst of all. But are you really humble like this in your own opinion? You easily compare yourself with this one and that one, but to how many do you not prefer yourself with the pride of the Pharisee: "I am not as the rest of men" (Luke 18;11). When you prefer yourself to others, it often seems as if you speak with a certain humility and modesty, saying, "By the grace of God, I have not the vices of such a one; By the grace of God I have not committed so many grievous sins as such a one." But is it really true that you recognize that you owe all this to the grace of God and that you give Him the glory rather than to yourself? If you esteem yourself more highly than such a one, and if he in his turn esteems himself inferior to you, he is therefore humbler than you, and for that reason better.[32]

But how do you practically help your child become humble towards others? After all, your child is legitimately better at many things than others. How do you navigate the young mind towards humility? Father Cajetan, the author of *Humility of Heart,* cites St. Thomas in providing four

---

[32]   Ibid., pp. 157–58.

ways to help us practice humility towards others. I have adapted these four ways to the act of parenting:

1. Impress upon your child's mind that he *owns* the vices and that God *owns* the virtues. Children do not mind, I promise you, giving God the credit for their strengths—only adults do. Then, focus the child's mind on the general blessings that the neighbor possesses as a gift from God, such as human dignity.

2. Help your child find some particular good quality in the other person that your child lacks. This takes creativity on your part, but if you set your mind to it, you will have one of the most fascinating conversations with your child.

3. Do the inverse. Lead your child to admit a fault of his own that the other person lacks. Again, an amazing insight will arise from your child—and your heart as a parent will be lifted. Lovingly agreeing with your child about his shortcomings is a remarkable thing—a liberating truth, a bonding between parent and child. Your souls will look at each other like never before.

4. Lastly, you must do the difficult task, especially as your child ages, of warning him that a secret pride might be lurking deep within his soul, so

deep and treacherous that he is not aware of its presence. Yes, you must instill a deep awareness in your child of the devil's cunning and guile.

In conclusion, Christian Parent, you cannot give what you do not have. If you practice this very exercise towards your own enemies, you will be better equipped to instruct your child in the ways of humility.

Towards Self

If you dare, ask yourself:

- Do you consider yourself virtuous because you perform little charitable acts here and there?
- Are you impressed with your own devotional life or knowledge of the Faith?
- Are you confident in your own ability to figure out moral problems?
- Do you fish for others' compliments?
- Do you feel good when others compliment you, or do you feel ashamed that they do not know the viciousness of your own sins?
- Do you use your words to prove others wrong?

- Does your mind quickly critique another person, or do you patiently seek the good in what the other person says?
- Do you find yourself criticizing another person behind their back? And have you really considered the incredible burdens that they carry and difficulties they have overcome?
- Are you quick to give your opinion to others as if you know better than them, and do you welcome the opportunity to share your knowledge with others?
- Are you a little too impressed with your looks, your clothing, your style? And are you quick to draw conclusions about others based on their appearance?

An examination of conscience according to the virtue of humility could be extremely lengthy and burdensome. However, making an extensive list for yourself and your child is certainly worth the effort, for no one becomes a saint without seeking to eradicate pride. Far too often you admit, "Yes, I struggle with pride." Oh, but is it not pride that prevents you from digging deep? How much would you benefit from hours upon hours of reflection on just how pride infects every area of your life: how you walk, talk, think, work, teach, listen, eat, sleep? Pride, my Dear Parent, is so insidious that it is present in every aspect of your life. And the moment you are aware of your own small improvements in your humility, you become prideful about your own humility! This is precisely why the truly humble man or woman actually—literally—believes that they are the most wretched of creatures.

After your child has learned the basics of a good confession but before the teenage years begin, sit down with your child and go through every area of life to examine the presence of pride. Truly, a great act of humility on your part would be to share some of your own prideful sins. In fact, the surest way for our children to be truly humble is if you, Dear Parent, are truly humble. A prideful child is often the fruit of haughty parents.

You want your child to be analytical in finance, in mathematics, in pursuing career options, but why not in the one realm that truly matters? Take every ounce of precision that your own mind can muster, combine it with passionate zeal for the state of your child's soul, and help your child learn, practically, how to search for hidden pride in every area of life. What a gift you can give your child!

And when your bones are humbly rotting in the ground, and your adult child is on his or her knees in the confessional, and is seeking absolution for the slightest prideful thought, desiring to root out every remnant of pride towards God and neighbor, God will reward you for a job well done.

A SENSE OF THE
COMPLETE CHURCH

The Protestant Reformation did not create freedom; it created anarchy. It opened wide the gates so that the entire flock, one by one, could wander through wastelands without a shepherd to guide them. Now, over five hundred years after one of the greatest tragedies the world has ever seen, the countless severing of one denomination from another has resulted in any one being able to set up "his own church." Can you imagine, Good Christian, the Apostles of Jesus Christ setting up "their own churches"? Jesus Christ founded one Church upon the Rock that is St. Peter, and all his fellow apostles knew it, even St. Paul.

It is, therefore, important for your child to grow up with a sense of the complete Church; this is not St. Ann's or St. Patrick's or All Saint's. No! Your child's Church is the one, holy, catholic, and apostolic Church. And your parish, or where you attend Holy Mass, happens to be this or that particular place.

And the complete Church has three parts: the Church Militant, the Church Suffering, and the Church Triumphant. Your child must know his or her place in this one, true Church while sojourning through the three states.

Church Militant

Militant is a word that modern parents do not appreciate. They believe Christianity to be all clouds and rainbows, void of anything harsh, and certainly without any notion of fighting or violence. Do not fall into this devilish trap, Dear Parent! Your child is, indeed, part of a military: the greatest military of the Divine Majesty. Your son, your daughter, is a soldier sent to fight God's enemies, the legions of darkness, the demons of hell. If you cringe at such a reality, Dear Parent, you must pause and reflect on your own understanding of the fallen world in which we live. There was, before the beginning of time, a cosmic battle between Lucifer and the fallen angels versus St. Michael and the faithful angels. This is a vicious war, a war that puts all human bloodshed to shame. And it is the continual war over the souls of mankind. Tradition holds that Lucifer could not stand the idea of bowing before the flesh and blood of the Infant Jesus, and so he led a revolt to which all human revolutions pale in comparison.

This war between good and evil has been cast upon your little child. Your child has no choice but to put on the armor of God, to go headlong into the breach, and to offer his life and limb for the King.

And what role do you play? Not only are you a member of the army but you have been called to train your troops in the ways of God's soldiery. Yes, you are the primary educators of this little soldier. You must shape his mind not only in the ways of the Lord but in the ways of spiritual battle. Your child must know the enemy, and thus hiding Satan's reality only sets him up for a surprise attack.

You must also train your child, body and soul. That is right: *body* and soul. Your little soldier must learn to endure physical pain, as every soldier must do in the drudgery of trench warfare. You will train your little one through fasting and abstinence, not only in Lent, but in Advent, and on every Friday for the rest of his life. You will train your child to offer up bodily suffering, and such training begins with skinned knees and rumbling tummies. You must look at your child and say, "I'm sorry you are hurt, but find the strength to offer up your suffering to Our Lord." This will be difficult for such a loving parent as you are. But seize the moment! When your child is leaning over the toilet, sick with the stomach bug, do not just hand over a towel and rub his back, but call the soldier forth to training. Gently remind your child to offer his suffering for this or that child with cancer or for this or that child who is going to bed hungry. There is never an inopportune time to creatively, gently, and affectionately train your child in the Divine Majesty's service.

You do not know if your child will one day command a great charge against the Church's visible and invisible foes, like St. Louis IX, or whether he will wage a silent, lifetime war in his own heart. But one thing is clear: there will be a battle. As a member of the Church Militant, there is no escaping it, for the enemies are attacking. And they will attack until your child finally enters the Church Suffering.

Church Suffering

Only in the Holy Catholic Faith can you fix your mind upon something so horrific yet marvelous, gruesome yet beautiful, that which you desperately want to avoid yet is that which you will one day willingly throw yourself into. That, Dear Parent, is the awesome reality of Purgatory, the residence of the Church Suffering.

It is difficult to believe that any thinking Christian can reject this doctrine. Do you want to know a truly appalling notion? It is that which is held by every Protestant: when you die, so long as you are not bound for hell, you get to immediately show yourself before the throne of Almighty God, with all the filth on your soul that venial sin has left,

King Louis IX before Damietta

without the need for penance, without any purification after a sinful life; and vastly more dreadful is the notion that a human soul would proudly walk before the throne of God among the blessed saints and angels without any thought of purgation.

Oh, how we clean our bodies, wash our clothes, polish our shoes, fix our hair, and adorn ourselves with jewelry, making ourselves as attractive as possible, simply to attend a cocktail party with halfwits and unscrupulous opportunists who care no more about us than their fancy allows for the fleeting moment.

And yet, we would presume to march into Paradise, the heavenly banquet, covered in the stench of pride, the rags of envy, with the growl of greed seething through clenched teeth, and the drool of gluttony seeping down our faces, with the blood of wrath on our hands, and the jaded look of sloth in our eyes, and yes, the filth of lust on display for all to see.

The glorious doctrine of Purgatory teaches, with countless apparitions to holy saints to support it, that the soul will be scandalized to present itself to God before it is purified in the fires of divine love.

A master of the spiritual life, Father Frederick Faber (1814–1863), explains this beautifully in the small but mighty book simply entitled *Purgatory*:

[The soul] goes into Purgatory with its eyes fascinated and its spirit sweetly tranquilized by the face of Jesus, its first sight of the Sacred Humanity, at the Particular Judgment which it has undergone. That vision abides with it still, and beautifies the uneven terrors of its prison as if with perpetual silvery showers of moonlight which seem to fall from our Savior's loving eyes. In the sea of fire it holds fast by that image. The moment that in His sight it perceives its own unfitness for Heaven, it wings itself voluntary flight to Purgatory, like a dove to her proper nest in the shadows of the forest. There need [be] no Angels to convey it thither. It is its own free worship of the purity of God.[33]

Father Faber also shares the incredible revelation of St. Gertrude, who was enraptured by God in the following scene:

The Saint saw in spirit the soul of a religious who had passed her life in the exercise of the most lofty virtues. She was standing before Our Lord clothed and adorned with charity, but she did not dare to lift her eyes to look at Him. She kept them cast down as if she was ashamed to stand in His presence, and showed by some gesture her desire to be far from Him. Gertrude marveled at this and ventured to question Him: "Most merciful God! Why does Thou not receive this soul into the arms of Thine infinite charity? What are the strange gestures of

---

[33]   Frederick Faber, *Purgatory* (Charlotte, NC: TAN Books, 2002), p. 18.

diffidence which I behold in her?" Then Our Lord lovingly stretched out His right arm, as if He would draw the soul nearer to Himself; but she, with profound humility and great modesty, retired from Him. The Saint, lost in still greater wonder, asked why she fled from the embraces of a Spouse so worthy to be loved; and the religious answered her, "Because I am not yet perfectly cleansed from the stains which my sins have left behind them; and even if he were to grant me in this state a free entrance into Heaven, I would not accept it; for all resplendent as I look to your eyes, I know that I am not yet a fit spouse for my Lord."[34]

And so it is a marvel that a Christian may think a sinful man can saunter right through the pearly gates. A truly humble soul desires purgation, knowing that despite the Blood of Christ spilt on Calvary, which made salvation possible, he continues to defile his soul in big ways and small.

Thus, Dear Parent, Purgatory is a glorious doctrine to teach your children, for it is a splendid means to prepare the soul for the Beatific Vision.

This beautiful notion of the soul's willingness to fly into the flames does not, in any way, diminish the brutality of the flames themselves. It has been reported by mystics throughout all of Church history—and even by the souls who have returned from the Church Suffering to warn the Church

---

[34] Ibid., pp. 18–19.

Militant—that the pain of purgation is greater than *all pains of earth combined*. It does not take a vivid imagination to conclude how painful this must be if we are incapable of holding our own hand over an open flame for even a few seconds. It is truly mind-boggling. It is, in fact, a mystery that the living cannot fathom. But you, Dear Parent, can listen to the warnings of the Holy Souls in Purgatory and teach your child about this beautiful and horrific reality.

It is vitally necessary to teach your little one to pray for the Poor Souls in Purgatory. They desperately desire it. Countless saints and mystics have testified to the importance of helping the Church Suffering. And even the Angelic Doctor, St. Thomas Aquinas, proclaimed that "prayer for the dead is more acceptable than for the living, for the dead are in the greatest need of it and cannot help themselves, as the living can."[35] An estranged friend, who has even left the Church, can freely choose to restore friendship with God and you. But our friends in Purgatory must rely on us for an earlier departure from the flames. Therefore, you and your family must pray for the dead with sincerity and devotion. It is yet another glorious mystery of God's infinite compassion that He gives the living such power over the dead.

Father Faber puts beautiful words to this notion:

---

[35] *Summa Theologiae*, Suppl. 3. Part, q. 71, art. 5 ad 3.

While we are helping the Holy Souls, we love Jesus with a love beyond words, a love that almost makes us afraid, yet with what a delightful fear! Because in this devotion it is His hands we are moving, as we would move the unskillful hands of a child. Dearest Lord, that He should let us do these things! That He should let us do with His satisfaction what we will, and sprinkle His Precious Blood as if it were so much water from the nearest well! That we should limit the efficacy of His unbloody Sacrifice, and name souls to Him, and expect Him to obey us, and that He should do so! Beautiful was the helplessness of His blessed Infancy; beautiful is His helplessness in His most dear Sacrament; beautiful is the helplessness in which, for the love of us, He mostly wills to be with regard to His dear spouses in Purgatory, whose entrance into glory His Heart is so impatiently awaiting! Oh, what thoughts, what feelings, what love should be ours as we, like choirs of terrestrial angels, gaze down on the wide, silent, sinless kingdom of suffering, and then, with our own venturous touch, wave the sceptered hand of Jesus over its broad regions, all richly dropping with the balsam of His saving Blood![36]

And so, Dear Parent, train your child to pray for the Poor Souls at every opportunity. At the conclusion of your mealtime, add the following prayer, "And may the souls of the

---

[36]   Frederick Faber, *Purgatory*, p. 14.

faithful departed, through the mercy of God, rest in peace."
Look for additional prayers to pray with your little one at
his or her bedtime routine. And when someone you know
or hear about passes away from the mortal coil, gather your
family together and pray one of the many prayers for the
faithful departed.[37]

If you raise your child to be mindful that members of his
Church are suffering in Purgatory at this very minute, you
will have done a great service. Convince your little one that
his prayers literally free the Holy Souls from their sufferings. Have your child imagine how grateful these souls will
be once they reach Heaven and how they will return the
favor through their prayers.

The point, Dear Parent, is that your child must have a
sense of the complete Church, not just the brick and mor-
tar building you attend on Sundays. How often do you
hear of someone in need of prayers? You discuss the person in need, you tell your friends and child, you add them
to your prayer list. And yet, the tradition proves time and
time again that the members of *your* Church are in Purgatory and need your prayers desperately, immediately. This

---

[37] In the back of the book often cited here, *Purgatory* by Father
Faber, there is a list of several prayers for the souls in Purgatory,
including a novena for each day of the week. I have included this
list of prayers in appendix 2.

is what it means to be member of the Church. Please, never let your child forget this truth.

Church Triumphant

Earlier in this work, we reflected on the glories of Heaven and the glorified body. And in subsequent chapters, we will reflect on the Blessed Mother, the angels, and the saints, all of whom are members of the Church Triumphant.

For the sake of brevity, I will only mention that as a parent, you must find creative ways to explain to your child that all in Heaven are Catholic. There are no Jews or Muslims, no Methodists or Baptists. There are only Catholics. Do not confuse what I am saying: this does not mean only practicing Catholics on earth go to Heaven, but it does mean that all who are saved are saved through the Catholic Church and that Purgatory is one long process of becoming truly Catholic. Jesus Christ formed one Church. And the Church Triumphant is the fullness of this Church. There is no room for any imperfect doctrine or denomination.

A story goes like this: Once upon a time, a young priest was visiting his father's deathbed. The priest was a convert. The father, however, remained anti-Catholic. "Don't you go saying one of those stupid Masses for me," the dying man said.

The young priest gave no reply but sat quietly in his sorrow.

"Promise me," the dying father said. "Promise me you won't say a Mass for me. I don't believe in that hocus-pocus."

The young priest looked at his father and said, "I promise, Dad, that I will not say a Requiem Mass for you unless you change your mind."

That very night, the old man died. The young priest held his father's hand and said, "Well, looks like you have now changed your mind."

Off the priest went to say the most beautiful Requiem Mass he could muster for his departed father.

The moral of the story, Dear Parents, is that all the souls in Heaven are fully and completely Catholic (and that the Church Suffering is one hell of an RCIA program). Instruct your child in seeing that Heaven is the fullness of his religion and that every step he walks in the Church Militant and endures in the Church Suffering will result, God willing, in his own glory in the Church Triumphant.

The Nativity

RELIANCE ON OUR LADY AND THE SAINTS

Giving your child a sense of belonging is of irreplaceable value. So many little ones grow up lost, even in a family. Perhaps they are neglected. Perhaps they are abused. Perhaps dad and mom are just tired.

And so, in addition to the natural means of making a child feel wanted and loved, such as family dinners, night prayers, playing together, physical affection, listening and talking, reading aloud, and so on, there is something even greater you can do. This, Dear Parent, is to instruct your child that Mary is our mother and the saints are our friends.

Your little child, so sweet and tender, is very capable of experiencing the affection of the Blessed Mother and the constant support of those saints in the Church Triumphant.

Mother Mary

It all begins with tenderness. The little ones need a mother's touch. And in our glorious religion, we have the supreme benefit of having an earthly mother and a heavenly one.

Fill your home with images of the Blessed Mother. As you carry your little one upstairs for bedtime, not only say good night to Daddy or the older siblings, but also stop at a sacred image of Our Lady and say good night to Mother Mary, or as some affectionately say, Mama Mary. Place an image of your child's Mama Mary in his room in addition to the most essential crucifix.

As your child matures into adolescence, clearly explain how the Blessed Mother is the model of purity. Her perpetual virginity is a sign of offering one's body to God as a noble sacrifice.

Tell your daughter, directly, to imitate the modesty of Mary in all her attire, in how she presents herself. Ask her how the Blessed Mother would approve of her behavior.

Tell your son, directly, to keep the purity of Mary in mind as he begins to interact with young women, and especially as he chooses a wife. Ask him if this or that girl reminds him of the Blessed Mother. And then tell him that if the answer is not an immediate *yes,* he should run from her as fast as his legs can take him.

When you, as father and mother, are totally spent—one more meal to cook, one more mess to clean, one more floor to sweep, one more diaper to change, one more toilet to plunge, one more drain to unclog, one more appliance to fix, one more insurance adjustment to make, one more bill to pay—remember the humility and charity that the Blessed Mother had when she served all those around her.

Yet again, the truth stares us in the face: your child's devotion to Our Lady will mirror your own. You must prepare a little place of refuge in your heart that belongs just to her and seek her intercession. With just one Hail Mary or one whispered "O Mary, conceived without sin, pray for us who have recourse to thee" you can fly to this place. Rest in the company of Mary, ask for her special graces, and be instantly refreshed—your humility and charity restored. And then, as you come away from your refuge, you will feel the very tenderness from our loving Mother, and in turn pass it on to your little one.

Familiarity with the Saints

A child deserves to grow up surrounded by the saints of Heaven. It is your duty, Good Parent, to feed their eyes with sacred images of the saints, their minds with sacred stories of the saints, and their hearts with sacred devotions to the saints. Your child should consider the saints as real as they consider aunts and uncles and friends; in fact, more so. If your little one complains that he has no friends, point to his heavenly companions, who are always more loyal than earthly friends.

It is important for you and your spouse—and perhaps your older children—to choose a patron saint of the family. Maybe it is glorious St. Joseph, but maybe it is a lesser-known saint who has meaning to your family. Choosing a patron saint should be an "event." Carve out the time; have the participants bring a list of candidates and provide a written reason for each one; put them on a board or on a master list. Discuss all of them. There are no wrong ideas when it comes to choosing a patron saint. Narrow it down to a handful. And then pray over it for a few days. Perhaps seek a holy priest's opinion. Once you have chosen, find a sacred image of this holy man or woman, study their lives attentively, and invoke his or her intercession frequently. The end of the Holy Rosary is an opportune time to ask them to "pray for us."

Additionally, choose your child's baptismal name carefully. Do not be too trendy—an unfortunate trap modern parents fall into. Choose a biblical or canonized saint's name. And then tell your child throughout his life that he has been entrusted to this saint by his very name. Again, have a sacred image of this patron saint right next to your child's bed. While not as precious as one's Guardian Angel, a patron saint is of great importance in the preservation of the Faith.

Furthermore, the properly formed family relies on the saints for all sorts of things. The Communion of Saints grants us the tremendous privilege to invoke their intercession in big things and small.

Your aim should be to form your child so that when they embark on a new task, challenge, endeavor, adventure, or suffering, they naturally ask, "Who is the patron saint of this?" If you have a little helper in the kitchen, tell them the story of St. Lawrence being grilled alive—and thus he is the patron of cooking! If your child is struggling with his school, tell him to pray to St. Benedict, patron of students. If your child can't find his shoes as he is running out the door, quickly remind him to invoke the intercession of St. Anthony. If you and your child are going on a hike, mending a broken fence, burying a dead dog, whatever the task may be, pull out your smart phone and search right then and there, "Who is the patron saint of _____."

The point, Dear Parent, is to use every opportunity to train that young mind in the ways of patron saints. It is a beautiful gift to give your children, one they will carry with them until they meet all those holy men and women of God in their own glory.

AWARENESS OF THE ANGELIC AND DEMONIC

Can't you see them? You, Dear Parent, can't you see the angelic and demonic all around? And why not? You *see* germs on a public water fountain. You *see* danger lying ahead in an empty street. You *see* sickness coming on the face of your little one even before an army of doctors could. You *see* attitude in the body language of your teenager that speaks only to you.

You *see* all kinds of things that are there, even if the naked eye doesn't actually see it. Your eyes are mere cameras, capturing light and darkness. Your soul, however, is able to capture far more than the material realm.

So I ask again: can't you see them, those countless angels governing the material universe? That is right. There is an angel that makes the world turn around, not unlike the ancient Greeks believed that Apollo in his chariot pulled the sun across the sky. There is an angel that holds the earth in space, not unlike Atlas did on his shoulders. God

Almighty assigns armies of angels to hold all the beautiful constellations of stars in their beautiful pattern in the sky, not unlike Zeus assigned the virgin goddess Astraia to the constellation Virgo.

Holy Mother Church has long taught that while God put the laws of nature into the universe, He likewise assigns angels to govern them. Truly, it is angelic power that enables gravity to keep your little one's feet firmly planted on the ground and keeps the planets in orbit around the sun.

In the inspiring book *St. Michael and the Angels*, we find a magnificent explanation of Church teaching on what has traditionally been called "The Empire of the Angels":

> According to St. Augustine, there are angels who preside over every visible thing and over each different species of creatures in the world, whether animate or inanimate. If God were to open our eyes and show us the angels under sensible forms, what wonders we should discover! Let us consider that all the comfort and benefit we derive from earth, air, water and fire, from the heavens, from animals – in fact from every creature, comes to us through the agency of the holy angels, who are God's faithful ministers.
>
> St. Thomas incidentally gives us another proof of angelic strength. He teaches that each great star, planet and sun, every heavenly body, even the greatest, has its own Guardian Angel to keep it in its course to and prevent

> any possible aberration. . . . To prevent disorder and
> confusion in the thousands of heavenly bodies whirling
> through space with inexpressible speed, God gives each
> one, in His all-wise Providence, an angel to keep it in
> its course and avert the dire calamities that would result
> were it to stray from its allotted orbit.[38]

Can you see them now? Yes, you must invoke your eyes of
faith. But they are there, Dear Parent. They are all around.

Next time you feed your little one a vegetable or fruit,
consider this: an angel used his own hands to mingle the
soil's nutrients and ushered them into the roots of the plant;
and another dangled his fingers, like a puppet master, to
make rain gently fall on the crops; and another whispered
into the minds of bees (for they do not have ears) to fly and
pollinate this plant and another. And as a great conductor
lifts his hands to raise the sound of the orchestra, another
angel called forth the sprouting of the plant, raising it from
the earth and into the very sunbeam that his brother angel
bore on his wings for ninety-two million miles.

There is no blessing in your life, Christian Reader, that
has not been touched by the hands, the wing tips, or the
hem of heavenly robes belonging to God's courtiers. Do
they not deserve your recognition? Your gratitude? Your
honor, praise, and devotion?

---

[38] *St. Michael and the Angels* (Charlotte, NC: TAN Books, 2012), p. 10.

The Choirs of Angels

Think how you honor your child's doctor, teacher, or godparents. And what have they done compared to the Guardian Angels who perform innumerable miracles just to keep your child alive one more day!

The Nine Choirs of Angels

Tradition holds that there are three hierarchies of Angels, each divided into three Choirs. This beautiful division is worthy of a short description of each. Just as you teach your child how to use the right tool for a certain job, you should teach your child how to invoke the best suited Choir of Angels for a particular intention. Do you not do this with the saints? When looking for a lost object, do you say, "Dear saints, help me find it!" or do you specifically invoke St. Anthony of Padua, patron saint of lost articles? Likewise, teach your child how to invoke a specific kind of angel for a specific intention. Not only is such invocation far more interesting, but it shows proper respect for their divinely given function in the order of salvation. And lastly, given the extraordinary gratitude you owe to your son or daughter's Guardian Angel, it is fitting that you learn extensively about his position in the heavenly court.

First Hierarchy

The first hierarchy is unique in its closeness to God.[39]

1. **Seraphim:** Their name means "ardor," or "passion." They sit right next to the throne of God, consumed by the fire of His love. Lucifer was a Seraphim. We should invoke the Seraphim to enkindle in us the sacred flame of love of God.

2. **Cherubim:** Far from chubby baby angels, their name means "fullness of knowledge," for they have deep insight into God's secrets. They speak God's wisdom to the other choirs. Invoke them to understand the deeper meanings of the Christian life.

3. **Thrones:** Their main characteristics are submission and peace, for peace comes from holy submission to the Divine Majesty. Invoke the Thrones for peace and holy submission in your home to the will of God.

Second Hierarchy

The second hierarchy is more devoted to the management of human affairs.

---

39   This outline is derived from *St. Michael and the Angels*, pp. 19–23, with minimal elaboration.

4. **Dominions:** Their name refers to their being responsible for executing the angelic orders given by the Great Monarch. The Dominions make known to you the commands of God. Invoke them for the strength to follow the commands of God during our earthly pilgrimage.

5. **Virtues:** These carry out the orders given by the Dominions. They also govern the seasons, the visible heavens, and the natural elements. You can thank them for the beauty of nature around you.

6. **Powers:** Known to be the favorite angels among mortals because the Powers are the primary fighters against demons and their wicked plans. There is a never-ceasing attempt by the powers of hell to destroy the Church and state for the sake of leading man astray. And the Powers of Heaven are traditionally invoked to defeat the devil's sinister plots upon the world.

Third Hierarchy

Similar to the second hierarchy, the third is dedicated to the visible world of men.

7. **Principalities:** Their primary role is to guard the nations of the earth. They should be in-

voked for protection of our country and for inspiring politicians to faithfully discharge their duties.

8. **Archangels:** They are entrusted with the most important missions of men. Thus, great personages, such as the Holy Father, cardinals, bishops, and even rulers of state (which would include the president) are given by God not just a Guardian Angel, but an archangel. St. Michael is the guardian of the Church and defends Her against demonic assaults. We should ask their protection over specific Church and state leaders.

9. **Angels:** Finally, the angels that are properly called Angels. These are the ordinary messengers sent to men by God. From these ranks come our own Guardian Angels. These are the ones protecting your little one throughout his life.

Familiarity with One's Guardian Angel

Look upon your little one. Your child's little veins are filled with flowing blood, but it is his Guardian Angel that gently pumps the heart in the palm of his hand. Your child's little neuropathways are growing and shaping each day like the most elaborate interstate system to carry data throughout his tiny body. But it is your child's Guardian Angel that directs all that traffic, ensuring that the lungs know to breathe, the eyes know to blink, the arms and legs know to move, and the tummy knows to rumble.

As a great cardinal of the Church once wrote:

> They never forsake us from the first breath we draw until we have entered into the possession of our eternal destiny. They hover about the babe slumbering in its crib, they guide the timid and untried steps with which childhood and youth enter upon life, as first so strange and at all times so full of perils. They hold out a helping hand to strong and rugged manhood, seasoned by struggles with the forces of evil, and bearing perhaps the scars which the wounds of sin have made. And when the light of life is transformed into the darkness and gloom of age, with its dreams unrealized and its hopes cherished in vain, Guardian Angels are near to support the bent form and tottering steps and to banish the shadows of loneliness and sorrow.[40]

As a parent, you owe your child's Guardian Angel tremendous honor, praise, and gratitude. But more importantly, you must teach your child to do the same.

---

[40]   Ibid., p. 16 (quoted from an uncited work by Cardinal O'Connell on the angels).

Teach your child to be aware of his Guardian Angel. Tell your child that the angel protected him during sleep. Tell your little one that when he falls and gets hurt, the angel saved him from greater pain and suffering. Tell your child how many times you saw him fall as a baby, how many close calls he experienced, how many times your own heart skipped a beat as he darted into a busy parking lot. And then tell your child it was his Guardian Angel that wrapped his wings around him, protecting your little one from the surrounding dangers.

The sentimental Christian and New Age world has reduced Guardian Angels to a childish fantasy, nothing more than a holy imaginary friend captured in children's artwork. But you, Dear Parent, must help your child develop a mature knowledge of the great glory, massive power, and blinding beauty of this heavenly creature assigned by God to your child. At some point when your child is old enough to comprehend, explain to him that if an angel were to appear, it might be mistaken for God Himself! Explain to your little one that an angel's magnificence is so great that one look would overload the human brain and bring us to instant death. Truly. This is the splendor of even the ninth choir of angels. Imagine the extraordinary humility of such a creature who can fly about the universe in a blink of an eye but gladly protects your child from scraping his knee or elbow. Truly, as a parent, you know how gross humanity can be, how dirty one's hands must get when we love a helpless human being. And the glorious Guardian Angel, so beyond our grotesque corporeal form, humbly stoops down to our level and joyfully cares for the helpless that you so dearly love.

Through creative means, foster in your child a personal affection for his Guardian Angel. Speak of him frequently. Pray to him together. Remind your little one as he grows older to constantly invoke the Guardian Angel's protection, and you will provide him with a lifelong companion that no human relationship can replace.

And when your child dies after living a holy life, he will most likely still owe a penance in Purgatory. Consider the Guardian Angels' service to the souls in Purgatory with the following noble thought: "During its shorter or longer sojourn in Purgatory, the Guardian Angel will often visit the soul to bring it relief and comfort. In the writings of the Holy Fathers, it is revealed that the angels descend to the altars of earth, and drawing the Precious Blood from the golden chalices during the thousands of holy Masses daily celebrated, they shower it like a beneficent dew upon the flames of Purgatory."[41]

And then upon your child's release from Purgatory, your little one will be met in joyous splendor by the very Guardian Angel who kept him safe throughout life and comforted

---

[41]   Ibid., p. 45.

him throughout purgation—and who will now escort your child into Paradise.

Never Relegate the Demonic

Consider, Good Parent, how concerned you are about predators roaming the world, looking for little innocent victims. Whether these predators are lurking in the shadows of a parking lot, eerily standing near a playground, ·or summoning your little one into an internet chat room, your good parental instincts are forever attuned to the dark reality in which we live.

A far worse predator, however, prowls throughout every nook and cranny of your child's life, like a wild animal awaiting the perfect moment to pounce upon the weakened prey. Worse yet, there is not a single predator, but countless predators that will go to any length to bring your child's soul into the eternal pit of hell, for misery loves company. The devil has already been defeated by the Blood of Christ; his time is running out to snatch souls. And so, in his few remaining minutes, he fights with all his strength and glories (for now) in his victories.

If you believe this is an exaggeration, hyperbole, or unnecessarily morbid, then all I can say is that the devil is winning his battle for your soul, and for the soul of your child. After all, the author of *The Art of War*, Sun Tzu, famously said, "Appear weak when you are strong." Satan does not want you to know his cunning, his prowess, his relentless effort. When he has gained a mile, he does not want you to even know you have lost an inch. Beware, Christian Reader, of any notion that trivializes the devil.

In other words, never—under any circumstance—relegate the demonic to a small corner of life. "It is a divine truth that these spirits of evil are invisibly present on earth. They inhabit the atmosphere about us and frequent the haunts [frequented places] of men: their homes, and shops and marts and places of pleasure. They are busy not merely in person, but also through their agents, whom they are to control with but little effort."[42]

And thus, St. Peter warns you, especially as a parent, "Be sober and watch: because your adversary the devil, as a roaring lion, goeth about seeking whom he may devour" (1 Pt 5:8).

How many parents make the grave and perhaps irreversible mistake of ignoring the reality of demons in their child's life! It is understandable that you do not want to dwell on darkness, especially with a little one. It is admirable that you desire only good things to fill the mind of an impressionable child. But do you not warn them about germs, about "strangers," about the physical danger of fire? Are you a cruel parent if you pop the little hand

---

[42]   Ibid., p. 48.

The Fall of the Rebel Angels

that continually turns on the stove or sticks a fork in an electric socket? Yet again, you are so inclined to care for the body, even if it means putting your loved one through discomfort. But when it comes to the spiritual realm, you diminish the severity of the situation. This, My Friend, you will regret in the next life when your eyes are affixed on an eternal timeline rather than on this earthly time that is no greater than a drop of water in the vastness of oceans.

As a parent, you must teach your little one that the devil is real, that he was the greatest of angels, and that he fell from Heaven due to his rebellion and prideful refusal to worship the God-man. And he took a third of the angels with him. God's punishment for them was severe, for their culpability was nearly boundless; their knowledge of God's majesty was direct and immediate, but their pride was greater still.

You must teach your little one that demons are using the media to influence souls: a little violence here, and a little lust there. All so subtle until subtlety is no longer needed.

You must teach your teenager that lack of piety, sloppy prayers, and slothful attention at Holy Mass are all fodder for the snares of the devil.

You must teach your college student that the modern university is a cesspool of demonic activity: the leftist professors are agents of Satan's ideology; the unapologetic impurity of co-ed dorms is nothing more than a hotbed of diabolic orgy; and if he or she is going to survive this heinous environment unscathed, then a herculean effort in the devotional, sacramental, and liturgical life is required. Otherwise, your child will be another data point in the statistics of former Catholics.

If you have not raised your child with such awareness of the diabolical, the all-knowing young adult will roll his eyes and return to his socialist literature professor for insight. And so, Dear Parent, take every opportunity as your child grows to help him see the true spiritual warfare raging around him. The truth shall, indeed, set him free from the treachery of the demonic.

THE SCHOOL OF CALVARY

Stop. Be still. Calm the mind for a moment; allow the striking, jarring, chilling words of the God-man to sink deeply into your soul: "And he that taketh not up his cross, and followeth me, is not worthy of me" (Mt 10:38). "And calling the multitude together with his disciples, he said to them: If any man will follow me, let him deny himself, and take up his cross, and follow me" (Mk 8:34).

The Necessity of the Cross

As a Catholic, you have heard these lines countless times. If you are like most, however, they roll off of you like beads of water, never soaking in. Perhaps the greatest paradox of our divinely given faith is the torture and death of the God-man on a wooden cross. And the paradox continues to His followers: we must, metaphorically, die on our own crosses in order to be saved. We must follow Christ in the way of the cross. You, Loving Parent, *must* educate your little one in the school of Calvary. You must teach him to die little deaths, to never fear suffering, and to willingly and zealously pick up his cross and bear it with a heart bursting with love.

How counterintuitive this is for a loving parent! You spend your life helping your child avoid pain and suffering. You doctor the skinned knee; you brush and floss to avoid cavities; you strap a helmet on the little head to go along with the first bike.

But there is another form of suffering that you must teach your child to endure from the earliest ages. Look around at the modern man and woman: you will see that we live in the era of wimps. Men have become effeminate. The world will tempt your sons to become effeminate. Did you know that St. Paul addressed this very issue? "Know you not that the unjust shall not possess the kingdom of God? Do not err: neither fornicators, nor idolaters, nor adulterers, *nor the effeminate*, nor liers with mankind, nor thieves, nor covetous, nor drunkards, nor railers, nor extortioners, shall possess the kingdom of God" (1 Cor 6:9–10; emphasis added).

In a powerful book for men entitled *The Terror of Demons: Reclaiming Traditional Catholic Masculinity*, the author says, "The Greek word for 'effeminacy' in the New Testament is *malakia* (μαλακία) which means 'softness.' St. Thomas defines effeminacy as a reluctance to suffer due to an attachment to pleasure. He explains that effeminacy is a vice opposed to perseverance. In essence, effeminacy is a vice that is opposed to the Cross, which is an unfortunate characteristic that might explain the multitude of soft men who reject life's redemptive sufferings in pursuit of temporal pleasure."[43]

Perhaps my large number of children has spared me from the ability to spoil them. Perhaps I am too lazy to do so. But whatever the reason, I am astounded at how my peers, especially fathers, go to extreme lengths to make life easy for their children. Whether they are spoon feeding a child who can feed himself, doing dishes for a child who can reach the sink, folding laundry for a middle schooler, or paying good money to repair something that the teenager can figure out how to repair online, the modern parent often seeks to remove crosses from his or her child's path. On a natural level, there is a reason that children who grow up on a farm become more self-reliant, disciplined, and conservative adults—not expecting special treatment or government assistance to obtain their own success. Whether you live on a hundred acres or in a city apartment, you must force your child to do what he can do for himself.

Why do parents so often coddle their child? One possibility that you must reflect upon: they fear their child does not have sufficient respect for their authority and will thus

---

[43]   Kennedy Hall, *Terror of Demons: Reclaiming Traditional Catholic Masculinity* (Our Lady of Victory Press, 2020), p. 33.

revolt at the first sign of conflict. If you find yourself in this situation with, say, a teenager, you have perhaps failed for many years up to this point. Understandably, you cannot suddenly become a domineering force in the life of someone who has been allowed to walk all over you. The task before you is difficult; it is, in fact, one of conversion. And if you conclude that you have failed in your duties up to this point, you should confess your sins of omission to a priest. "Bless me, Father, for I have sinned. I have been a doormat to my kid for over seventeen years, and now I must walk on eggshells to even influence him." This, my Dear Parent, is a good confession. The sacramental grace you will receive through the priest will enable you to navigate the rough waters ahead.

As a parent, you must find little ways to make your child tough—on both the natural and supernatural level. Regarding the latter, be a constant reminder to your child that suffering is redemptive. Be creative: relate the physical suffering to spiritual development. When your son is complaining of doing yard work, tell him, "You must pull weeds from the garden just as you must pull up every venial sin in your life. See how fast that weed has grown and how it is covering the healthy plants? Selfishness and laziness and greed and lust all grow quickly and spread throughout every area of your life. Now go, pull those weeds like you mean it, and consider your sins while you do so." Or when

Insults for Christ During His Trial

your middle school daughter complains about doing the dishes, tell her what St. Teresa of Calcutta said: "Wash the dish not because it is dirty nor because you are told to wash it, but because you love the person who will use it next." Or when your high schooler gripes about doing the laundry, have the wherewithal to say, "Clothing the naked is one of the seven corporal works of mercy. And Jesus said, 'For I was hungry, and you gave me to eat; I was thirsty, and you gave me to drink; I was a stranger, and you took me in: *Naked, and you covered me:* sick, and you visited me: I was in prison, and you came to me' (Mt 25:35–36). In other words, child, don't waste your chores! Do them for Jesus, and you will have your reward in Heaven."

Yes, as a parent, you must get creative. But the law has an old adage: *you cannot give what you do not have.* Do you, Dear Parent, keenly understand that if you feed and clothe your child and care for him when he is sick—with the love of Christ—that you are feeding Him, clothing Him, and doctoring Him? Do you see these small burdens in your life as not only carrying your own cross but helping Jesus carry His, as did Simon of Cyrene? Or do you struggle through the daily chores, rushing the kids off to bed so that you can cast off all those little crosses, toss Jesus to the side, and return to your streaming video? A practical parent might say, "If you have to do the chore anyway, you might as well get some grace by offering it up!" A saintly parent, however,

does not do so out of utility to their own spiritual investment portfolio. No! A saint carries the little crosses out of
passionate, zealous charity for God and neighbor. At a certain point, self-interest vanishes, as a mother who forgets
herself and runs to the fallen child out of instinctual love.
There is no calculation of how taking on a little suffering
will benefit her. She cares nothing about dirtying her dress
when she kneels to the ground to help her child. She cares
not if her hair gets disheveled. She moves out of love, not
for a return on her investment.

You must learn to suffer out of love: unabashed, brazen,
barefaced love. You must first suffer for your spouse. And
when you feel the prick of self-love—the need for acknowl-
edgment or accolade, credit or compliment—be ashamed.
How did Christ at the column seek flattery while His flesh
was ripped from His bones by the flagrum? How did the
King of kings seek tribute as He was mocked with a crown
of thorns driven into His head?

In one of the greatest books ever written on the Passion,
ever-so aptly entitled *The School of Jesus Crucified: The Lessons of Calvary in Daily Catholic Life* (for as a parent, you
are the primary teachers of your child in the school of Calvary), we find a powerful meditation on Christ's willingness to suffer humiliation. As you read the following, ask
yourself why your ego is so easily wounded, how quickly

you take offense, how unworthy you are to be called a student of Jesus Crucified:

The enemies of Jesus Christ seem to take peculiar satisfaction in making Him a mock King, in ridiculing His sufferings, and in subjecting Him to every species of degradation and insult. They furiously tear off His garments, and clothe Him in a ragged purple mantel. This outrage is a source of exquisite suffering to Jesus, for the tearing off His garments re-opens all the wounds which have been so lately inflicted by His flagellation, so that fresh blood flows from the lacerated limbs. Oh, how much have the pleasures of our sinful flesh, the delicacy of our bodies, the luxury and vanity of our clothing, cost our sweet Jesus!

They place in His hand a reed as a scepter, to constitute Him a mock King, a King of a theater! Jesus refuses it not, but receives and holds it in His hand, rejoicing by so great a dishonor to merit for you graces of strength and perseverance in virtue, and to purchase for you a heavenly kingdom. In this state Jesus appears to the insolent soldiery a proper subject for mockery, and they proceed to ridicule him in a manner worthy of their cruelty. They all march before Him, saluting Him in the most derisive terms King of the Jews. They deride Him as a wretched imposter, adding shameful insults and reproaches to the most humiliating expressions of scorn and ridicule; they spit in His face, give Him blows, and, taking the reed out of His hand, strike the crown of thorns with it so violently as to enlarge every wound, and cause Him the most exquisite pain. They vie with each other in deriding and insulting Him, and in rendering His sufferings yet more cruel and ignominious. Oh, how ingenious is human cruelty in torturing Jesus! But in the meantime, His most holy Soul, though overwhelmed with the weight of so much ignominy and suffering, rejoices in offering to His Eternal Father the sacrifice of humiliations so profound, in reparation of the outrages offered to His Majesty by our sins. Bow down in adoration before this Divine King, return Him thanks for His infinite charity, and promise that you will love Him alone for the remainder of your life.

Amid his bitterest sufferings and most excessive humiliations, Jesus never once opens His mouth to complain. A frightful crown of thorns pierces His head on every side, and causes Him the acutest pain, yet he makes not the slightest complaint of the cruelty of His enemies. What do you say to this example of divine and superhuman patience, O you who are ever seeking after worldly pleasures and sensual gratifications, and who cannot endure even the slight thorn of some small inconvenience or trifling pain? You ought indeed to feel ashamed of living in luxury, when you behold your king, your Creator, and your God crowned with sorrow and ignominy. Do you calculate upon entering Heaven crowned with the roses of pleasure instead of thorns of mortification, suffering, and penance? Deceptive hope! Jesus Christ beholds Himself abandoned by all—in the power of His cruel enemies, outraged, defied with spittle, buffeted, and smitten, yet He maintains peace of soul, and calmness of demeanor, and makes not the slightest gesture of anger or impatience. *And you, wretched worm of the earth, unworthy sinner—you have not yet learned to submit in peace and silence to an insult, injury, or wrong done you by your neighbors! Is it possible that the sight of a God thus loaded with ignominy and suffering, and yet so patient and so humble, should not be sufficient to teach you patience and humility? If you do not imitate the example of Jesus Christ, you will not partake of his glory.*[44]

This, Good Parent, is the School of Jesus Crucified. And if you have not learned the way, it is all the more difficult to teach the way.

Ask yourself, was Jesus making an investment into His own glory? Or was He not suffering the unimaginable for your sake, and your child's sake, as an oblation, a final blood offering, to His Father in a pure act of unabashed, brazen, barefaced love? That, my Dear Reader, is the love of the cross. Paradise has no mansions for the utilitarian, for the calculating, for the Cyrenian who has a price.

---

[44] Ignatius of the Side of Jesus, *The School of Jesus Crucified: The Lessons of Calvary in Daily Catholic Life* (Charlotte, NC: TAN Books, 2012), pp. 122–24; emphasis added.

Husband: does your love of your wife have a price? How much appreciation must she give you for you to love her as Christ loves His Church? What is your minimum price? Must she stroke your ego at least once a month for you to die small deaths for her? Once a week? A day? From one man to another, I hope such a question torments you as it does me.

And wife: does your love for your husband have a price? Just exactly how much weight must he carry around the house to warrant your respect? What is your docility worth? Is doing 17 percent of the household work an equitable consideration for your feminine devotion, or do you draw the line at 32 percent? I pray you will contemplate unconditional love the next time you are tempted to negotiate through the sacrament of Matrimony.

Yes, you cannot give what you do not have. You cannot raise your child to love his or her cross until you love your own. Your son will learn the Way of the Cross by watching his dad joyfully maneuver through mom's mood or hypercriticism. Your daughter will learn the Way of the Cross by watching mom affectionately walk dad back from sinful bursts of anger or patiently pushing him out of his slothful slumber. You, Father and Mother, are the walking, breathing, bleeding Stations of the Cross. And if you fail in this moral duty, your soul is in the most severe jeopardy of eternal damnation. Why? Because the God-man said, "And he

Simon Helps Jesus with the Cross

that taketh not up his cross, and followeth me, *is not worthy of me"* (Mt 10:38; emphasis added).

Thus, if you have failed in your duty to instruct your little one in the Way of the Cross, you have most assuredly and woefully led your child astray. And it is better that a millstone be tied around your neck and that you be cast into the depths of the sea (see Mt 18:6; Mk 9:41; Lk 17:2). If three Gospels quoting the same divine warning is not enough, I am not sure what is.

The earthly reward, however, can be sweet if God so wills it. As your children grow, you will learn they respect you not for the pleasures you provide, but for the suffering you willingly endured for them and with them—and most assuredly—completely apart from them. Those little eyes see and have sympathy for the involuntary sufferings you endure. But they watch, internalize, memorize, and imitate the voluntary sufferings you endure. Little minds know that dad and mom did not have to make that sacrifice. They know dad does not have to wake up early to say his prayers. They know mom does not have to turn the cell phone off to read Scripture for five minutes in quiet. They know. They know the family does not have to load up screaming kids and go to confession frequently. They know. And they will love you for it. They will want to be like you. And one day, when you "catch" your young adult going to Eucharistic Adoration, you will feel the tenfold return of your many sacrifices—yes, even in this life if God so wills it.

Penance and Mortification

The modern world has made a mockery of penance and mortification. One of the direct results of the Protestant Reformation was the implicit rejection of an incarnational faith, with notions of "faith alone," and the explicit rejection of indulgences. The skeptic cannot fathom earthly actions, in the form of monetary sacrifice or physical mortification, being acceptable offerings to the Father in remission for the suffering souls in Purgatory.

The Enlightenment followed, further ingratiating the modern Christian with enlightened reason in place of medievalism's blind faith; one should think their way to truth rather than wallow in the muck of self-denial. "Tame the mind rather than tame the body!" the heresy of modernism would say, or has said.

Dear Parent, understand that the modern American culture in which you have been raised is like warm water, and you are the frog. With every passing decade, the temperature has been turned up. Our nation, with many blessings indeed, was founded by men of the Enlightenment. They were largely anti-Catholic rationalists with smidgens of Christian faith remaining here and there. It was the author of our Declaration of Independence, Thomas Jefferson, who committed the blasphemous, idolatrous mortal crime of publishing *The Life and Morals of Jesus of Nazareth*, commonly known as the *Jefferson Bible*. This Enlightenment scoundrel, whom we scandalously christen as a Founding Father, removed all signs of the miraculous and supernatural in order to promote Jesus as a wise man—a man of whom the Enlightenment would be proud—rather than as the Savior who died for him. This, Good Parent, is the America in which you live.

And thus, you should not be surprised that the progeny of such men reject all notions of a Christianity that is corporeal, physical, and bloody.

We Catholics glory in the flesh! We place little bits and pieces of flesh and bone in golden reliquaries, giving places of honor to the remnants of saints to reside with us. We dig up graves to see how much bodies have decayed in order to help assess a candidate for sainthood. We secretly wear hair shirts.[45] We strap on cilices high up our thighs, quietly enduring the pain of little metal pricks digging into our skin without anyone ever knowing. We walk the *Camino de Santiago*—all five hundred miles of it. We process on our knees around Marian shrines. We fast. We abstain. And why do we do these crazy things? Precisely because

---

[45]   Prudence and humility demand that such mortification be performed under supervision of a holy priest.

we believe in the resurrection and glorification of the very bodies that we seek to tame.

And you must teach your child how to tame his flesh *now* before the world teaches him how to indulge it and infects him with Protestant and Enlightenment ideals that diminish the role of the flesh in our salvation.

Diminish the role of the flesh in our salvation? What could be more blind to the truth! We are called to imitate Our Lord who became flesh and dwelt among us (see Jn 1:14). He did not, however, become just any flesh. He did not take the form of royalty, or of dainty Enlightenment bureaucrats reaching for their powdered wigs or their aged bottles of wine. Rather, He took on the form of humanity's broken and rejected flesh, the form of a slave (see Phil 2:7). His life, not just His passion, was filled with suffering, for God intended for our faith to be corporeal, not purely spiritual.

Remember, your child is not an angel. In fact, it was the Incarnation that drove Lucifer and his angels to rebel; they could not imagine worshiping the Word, Who became flesh, nor bowing before His mother. If your child is not raised in an incarnational faith, he will eventually reject the helpless, Infant Savior, just as Lucifer did.

And so what will your response be? Find every opportunity to lead your child in sacrifice. Do not be lukewarm and merely pray more during Lent, but also renounce something difficult.

Real difficult. Do not treat Advent like one big Christmas season. Rather, treat it like the ninety-mile march through the desert to Bethlehem that it was for the Holy Family. Christmas does not begin until Christmas. Advent is a little Lent. Act like it. Offer something up, even during the countless Christmas parties. Fast from meat on Fridays. (Although few know this, abstinence from meat *or some other sacrifice* is still required on Fridays.) Find physically hard things to do, and let your little one know why you are doing it.

Most importantly, teach your child to accept involuntary suffering like a Christian. The next time your little one has a stomach bug, kindly ask him for whom he would like to offer up the suffering. The next time your child has a headache, gently call to mind the crown of thorns and help your little one to ease Christ's pain by uniting his suffering with His.

I cannot provide an exhaustive list of opportunities to teach penance and mortification because, frankly, life itself is supposed to be one continuous Lent, as St. Benedict once wrote. As a parent, you must see every moment of your child's life as an opportunity to make a sacrificial offering. This I promise: if you understand your child's entire life—body and soul—as an offering to the heavenly Father, and if you have the fortitude to speak the truth, then the instructional moments will present themselves several times a day. You will not seek them out; they will seek you out.

Dear Parent, you must consider whether you are afraid of teaching your child how to suffer. The younger your child is, the easier it is. But how will you instruct the older child, even the grown child, whom you have neglected in this regard? It begins with your own repentances for failing your child. Confess to a priest: "Bless me, Father, for I have sinned. I missed twenty-five years of opportunities to enroll my child in the School of Jesus Crucified." While you might have to explain yourself a bit to the priest, this, my Dear Reader, is a beautiful confession. But next, you must find the fortitude, overcoming the awkwardness, to preach to your adult child the truths of Calvary. If he rejects you, at least he will be confronted with truth and have the opportunity to accept it.

Oh, but so many well-intentioned parents bury the truth under guises of finessing their wayward child. Admittedly, a parent must be cunning in their dealings with a rebellious child. Often, a lack of faith and fortitude causes parents to soft peddle the truth. Nothing here should be interpreted as being heavy-handed. Truth in charity, always. But truth. Truth.

The truth, therefore, is that your child will not enjoy the glories of Heaven without being schooled in the classroom of Calvary. Suffering is necessary. Penance and mortification are necessary. It is the way. It is the way to eternal glory.

Angels & the Exaltation of the Cross

A JOYOUS CONCLUSION

This was a wearisome book. Fighting for your child's eternal salvation is a wearisome task. But there is no greater joy and responsibility in this life than raising your child in the arms of Holy Mother Church. Thus, we have yet another paradox in our Holy Faith.

This should come as no surprise, for our Holy Faith is filled with paradox: joy is found in suffering; eternal life comes from the death of Christ; we must carry our crosses and yet Jesus's yoke is easy, and His burden is light; the Lord lifts up the lowly, and those who mourn shall be comforted. The paradoxes pour off the biblical page like the waters of Baptism.

Dear Parent, understand that it is not Heaven that is upside down, but the world; it is not the Church that is backwards, but her enemies.

Embrace the paradox: do not parent for this world, but for the world to come; do not prepare your little one for this life, but for the life to come; do not parent for time, but for eternity.

If you begin to live the contents of this little book, an indescribable joy will permeate your family life. Hear me: *everything* in your life will be forcibly changed: your marriage, your work, your friendships, your finances, and your entertainment. Yes, your entire life will no longer be the same: your joy will give rise to gratitude; your sorrow will increase your compassion; your sickness will become a source of sacrifice and your victories a source of humility; time with others will be a chance to speak about God and time alone will be a chance for God to speak to you.

Above all, your relationship with that little, immortal soul in your care will change. Your little one will see a joy radiate from you like he has never seen before. And it is this joy that becomes the greatest teacher of all.

Dear Parent: the very last thing I implore you to do is this: imagine meeting your son or daughter in Paradise, knowing that you will bask together in the glory of the Beatific Vision forever. Imagine, no more scraped knees, no more tummy aches, no more broken bones, no more broken hearts, no more temptation, no more sin, no more sickness, and no more death. All will be whole. All will be complete. All will be perfect. All will be for eternity. This is your purpose. Now go forth, parenting for eternity.

CHRIST'S FIFTEEN WARNINGS ON HELL

I

"Woe to the world because of scandals. For it must needs be that scandals come: but nevertheless woe to that man by whom the scandal cometh. And if thy hand, or thy foot scandalize thee, cut it off, and cast it from thee. It is better for thee to go into life maimed or lame, than having two hands or two feet, to be cast into everlasting fire. And if thy eye scandalize thee, pluck it out, and cast it from thee. It is better for thee having one eye to enter into life, than having two eyes to be cast into hell fire" (Mt 18:7–9).

II

"And if thy right eye scandalize thee, pluck it out and cast it from thee. For it is expedient for thee that one of thy members should perish, rather than that thy whole body be cast into hell. And if thy right hand scandalize thee, cut it off, and cast it from thee: for it is expedient for thee that one of thy members should perish, rather than that thy whole body be cast into hell" (Mt 5:29–30).

III

"And fear ye not them that kill the body, and are not able to kill the soul: but rather fear him that can destroy both soul and body in hell" (Mt 10:28).

IV

"The rich man also died: and he was buried in hell. And lifting up his eyes when he was in torments, he saw Abraham afar off, and Lazarus in his bosom: And he cried, and said: Father Abraham, have mercy on me, and send Lazarus, that he may dip the tip of his finger in water, to cool my tongue: for I am tormented in this flame" (Lk 16:22–24).

V

"Then he shall say to them also that shall be on his left hand: Depart from me, you cursed, into everlasting fire which was prepared for the devil and his angels" (Mt 25:41).

VI

"And I say to you that many shall come from the east and the west, and shall sit down with Abraham, and Isaac, and Jacob in the kingdom of Heaven. But the children of the kingdom shall be cast out into the exterior darkness: there shall be weeping and gnashing of teeth" (Mt 8:11–12).

VII

"The king went in to see the guests: and he saw there a man who had not on a wedding garment. And he saith to him: Friend, how camest thou in hither not having a wedding garment? But he was silent. Then the king said to the waiters: Bind his hands and feet, and cast him into the exterior darkness: there shall be weeping and gnashing of teeth" (Mt 22:11–13).

VIII

"The unprofitable servant cast ye out into the exterior darkness. There shall be weeping and gnashing of teeth" (Mt 25:30).

IX

"But I say to you, that whosoever is angry with his brother, shall be in danger of the judgment. And whosoever shall say to his brother, Raca, shall be in danger of the council. And whosoever shall say, Thou fool, shall be in danger of hell fire" (Mt 5:22).

X

"The Son of man shall send his angels, and they shall gather out of his kingdom all scandals, and them that work iniquity. And shall cast them into the furnace of fire: there shall be weeping and gnashing of teeth" (Mt 13:41–42).

XI

And if thy hand scandalize thee, cut it off: it is better for thee to enter into life, maimed, than having two hands to go into hell, into unquenchable fire: Where their worm dieth not, and the fire is not extinguished. And if thy foot scandalize thee, cut it off. It is better for thee to enter lame into life everlasting, than having two feet, to be cast into the hell of unquenchable fire: Where their worm dieth not, and the fire is not extinguished. And if thy eye scandalize thee, pluck it out. It is better for thee with one eye to enter into the kingdom of God, than having two eyes to be cast into the hell of fire: Where their worm dieth not, and the fire is not extinguished" (Mk 9:42–47).

XII

"Every tree that bringeth not forth good fruit, shall be cut down, and shall be cast into the fire" (Mt 7:19).

XIII

"I am the vine: you the branches: he that abideth in me, and I in him, the same beareth much fruit: for without me you can do nothing. If any one abide not in me, he shall be cast forth as a branch, and shall wither, and they shall gather him up, and cast him into the fire, and he burneth" (Jn 15:5–6).

XIV

"But Jesus turning to them, said: Daughters of Jerusalem, weep not over me; but weep for yourselves, and for your children. For behold, the days shall come, wherein they will say: Blessed are the barren, and the wombs that have not borne, and the paps that have not given suck. Then shall they begin to say to the mountains: Fall upon us; and to the hills: Cover us. For if in the green wood they do these things, what shall be done in the dry?" (Lk 23:28–31).

The Beatific Vision

XV

"You serpents, generation of vipers, how will you flee from the judgment of hell?" (Mt 23:33).

APPENDIX 2

PRAYERS & NOVENA FOR THE HOLY SOULS

A Prayer for the Souls in Purgatory

O Most gentle Heart of Jesus, ever present in the Blessed Sacrament, ever consumed with burning love for the poor captive souls in Purgatory, have mercy on the souls of Thy departed servants. Be not severe in Thy judgments, but let some drops of Thy Precious Blood fall upon the devouring flames. And do Thou, O Merciful Savior, send Thy holy angels to conduct them to a place of refreshment, light and peace. Amen.

A Prayer for Our Dear Departed

O Good Jesus, Whose loving Heart was ever troubled by the sorrows of others, look with pity on the souls of our dear ones in Purgatory. O Thou Who didst "love Thine own," hear our cry for mercy, and grant that those whom Thou hast called from our homes and hearts may soon enjoy everlasting rest in the home of Thy Love in Heaven. Amen.

V. Eternal rest grant unto them, O Lord.
R. And let perpetual light shine upon them. Amen.

A Prayer for Deceased Parents

O God, Who hast commanded us to honor our father and our mother, in Thy mercy have pity on the souls of my father and mother, and forgive them their trespasses, and make me to see them again in the joy of everlasting brightness. Through Christ Our Lord. Amen.

A Prayer for a Deceased Priest

O God, Thou didst raise Thy servant, N., to the sacred priesthood of Jesus Christ, according to the Order of Melchisedech, giving him the sublime power to offer the Eternal Sacrifice, to bring the Body and Blood of Thy Son Jesus Christ down upon the altar, and to absolve the sins of men in Thine own holy Name. We beseech Thee to reward his faithfulness and to forget his faults, admitting him speedily into Thy holy presence, there to enjoy forever the recompense of his labors. This we ask through Jesus Christ Thy Son Our Lord. Amen.

A Novena for the Poor Souls
By Father Frederick Faber

Sunday

O Lord God Almighty, I beseech Thee by the Precious Blood which Thy divine Son Jesus shed in the Garden, deliver the souls in Purgatory, and *especially that one which is the most forsaken of all,* and bring it into Thy glory, where it may praise and bless Thee forever. Amen.

Our Father . . . Hail Mary . . . Glory Be . . .
Eternal rest . . .

Monday

O Lord God Almighty, I beseech Thee by the Precious Blood which Thy divine Son Jesus shed in His cruel scourging, deliver the souls in Purgatory, and among them all, *especially that soul which is nearest to its entrance into Thy glory*, that it may soon begin to praise Thee and bless Thee forever. Amen.

Our Father . . . Hail Mary . . . Glory Be . . .
Eternal rest . . .

Tuesday

O Lord God Almighty, I beseech Thee by the Precious Blood of Thy divine Son Jesus that was shed in His bitter crowning with thorns, deliver the souls in Purgatory, and among them all, *particularly that soul which is in the greatest need of our prayers,* in order that it may not long be delayed in praising Thee in Thy glory and blessing Thee forever. Amen.

Our Father . . . Hail Mary . . . Glory Be . . .
Eternal rest . . .

Wednesday

O Lord God Almighty, I beseech Thee by the Precious Blood of Thy divine son Jesus that was shed in the streets of Jerusalem, whilst He carried on His sacred shoulders the heavy burden of the Cross, deliver the souls in Purgatory, and *especially that one which is richest in merits in Thy sight,* so that, having soon attained the high place in glory to which it is destined, it may praise Thee triumphantly and bless Thee forever. Amen.

Our Father . . . Hail Mary . . . Glory Be . . .
Eternal rest . . .

Thursday

O Lord God Almighty, I beseech Thee by the Precious Blood of Thy divine Son Jesus which He Himself, on the night before His Passion, gave as meat and drink to His beloved Apostles and bequeathed to His holy Church to be the perpetual sacrifice and life-giving nourishment of His faithful people, deliver the souls in Purgatory, but most of all, that soul which was most devoted to this Mystery of infinite love, in order that it may praise Thee thereof, together with Thy divine Son and the Holy Spirit in Thy glory forever. Amen.

Our Father . . . Hail Mary . . . Glory Be . . .
Eternal rest . . .

Friday

O Lord God Almighty, I beseech Thee by the Precious Blood which Jesus Thy divine Son did shed this day upon the tree of the Cross, especially from His sacred hands and feet, deliver the souls in Purgatory, and *particularly that soul for whom I am most bound to pray*, in order that I may not be the cause which hinders Thee from admitting it quickly to the possession of Thy glory, where it may praise Thee and bless Thee for evermore. Amen.

Our Father . . . Hail Mary . . . Glory Be . . .
Eternal rest . . .

Saturday

O Lord God Almighty, I beseech Thee by the Precious Blood, which gushed forth from the sacred side of Thy divine Son Jesus in the presence of and to the great sorrow of His most holy Mother, deliver the souls in Purgatory, and among them all, *especially that soul which has been most devout to this noble Lady*, that it may come quickly into Thy glory, there to praise Thee in her, and her in Thee, through all the ages. Amen.

Our Father . . . Hail Mary . . . Glory Be . . .
Eternal rest . . .

On Every Day of the Novena

V. O Lord, hear my prayer.
R. And let my cry come unto Thee.

APPENDIX 3

THE ANGELUS

V. The Angel of the Lord declared unto Mary.
R. And she conceived of the Holy Spirit.

Hail Mary, full of grace,
The Lord is with Thee;
Blessed art thou among women,
And blessed is the fruit of thy womb, Jesus.
Holy Mary, Mother of God,
Pray for us sinners,
Now and at the hour of our death. Amen

V. Behold the handmaid of the Lord.
R. Be it done unto me according to thy word.

Hail Mary, etc.

V. And the Word was made Flesh.
R. And dwelt among us.

Hail Mary, etc.

V. Pray for us, O holy Mother of God.

R. That we may be made worthy of the promises of Christ.

Let us pray.

Pour forth, we beseech Thee, O Lord, Thy grace into our hearts, that we to whom the Incarnation of Christ Thy Son was made known by the message of an angel, may by His Passion and Cross be brought to the glory of His Resurrection. Through the same Christ Our Lord. Amen.

APPENDIX 4

A PRAYER FOR YOUR CHILD'S VOCATION

Heavenly Father,
    You sent your Beloved Son to suffer and die so that my own beloved child can bask in your glory for all eternity.

Send your Holy Spirit upon my child that he might know his true vocation and give him the grace to follow it unreservedly.

Above all, keep my child from the fires of hell.

Guide me, O Lord, in teaching him to know, love, and serve you, through Jesus Christ Our Lord. Amen.

Hail Mary

ABOUT THE AUTHOR

Conor Gallagher is CEO of TAN Books and Executive Director of the Benedict Leadership Institute at Belmont Abbey College. He is the author of *If Aristotle's Kid Had an iPod: Ancient Wisdom for Modern Parents* and *Still Amidst the Storm: A Family Man's Search for Peace in an Anxious World*. He and his wife, Ashley, are the parents of fourteen children.

IMAGE CREDITS

Page 6 St. Peter denying Christ. Illustration for The Holy Bible with illustrations by Gustave Dore (Cassell, c 1880)/ Photo credit © Look and Learn / Bridgeman Images.

Page 28 The Prodigal Son in the arms of his father. Illustration for The Holy Bible with illustrations by Gustave Dore (Cassell, c 1880). Photo credit © Look and Learn / Bridgeman Images.

Page 41 The flight into Egypt. Illustration for The Holy Bible with illustrations by Gustave Dore (Cassell, c 1880). Photo credit © Look and Learn / Bridgeman Images.

Page 45 The baptism of Jesus. Illustration for The Holy Bible with illustrations by Gustave Dore (Cassell, c 1880).Photo credit © Look and Learn / Bridgeman Images.

Page 71 The Last Supper, Illustration from the Dore Bible / by Gustave Doré, 1832 - 1883, Lebrecht History / Bridgeman Images.

Page 79 Christ crucified, Illustration from the Dore Bible, 1866 / by Gustave Doré, 1832 - 1883, French / Bridgman Images.

Page 91 King Louis IX (1217-70) before Damietta, by Gustave Doré, 1832 - 1883, French. Illustration from 'Bibliotheque des Croisades' by J-F. Michaud, 1877 (litho) / Photo Ken Welsh / Bridgeman Images.

Page 100 The nativity, Birth of Christ in the manger, Illustration from the Dore Bible / by Gustave Doré, 1832 - 1883, Universal History Archive/UIG / Bridgeman Images.

Page 109 The Heavenly Choir, by Gustave Doré, 1832 - 1883, French. Engraving for Paradiso by Dante. Photo © Liszt Collection / Bridgeman Images.

Page 119 The Fall of the Rebel Angels, by Gustave Doré, 1832 - 1883, French. Engraving for Paradise Lost by Milton, Photo © Liszt Collection / Bridgeman Images.

Page 126 Insults for Christ during his trial, Illustration from the Dore Bible, 1866/ by Gustave Doré, 1832 - 1883, French Universal History Archive/UIG / Bridgeman Images.

Page 133 Jesus carries the cross, Illustration from the Dore Bible, 1866, Gustave Dore (1832-1883), French / Photo Universal History Archive/ UIG / Bridgeman Images.

Page 140 The Vision of the Cross, by Gustave Doré, 1832 - 1883, French. Engraving for the Purgatorio or Purgatory by Dante Alighieri. 1870, Photo © Liszt Collection / Bridgeman Images.

Page 148 Paradiso, Canto 31: Illustration from 'The Divine Comedy' by Dante Alighieri, by Gustave Doré, 1832 - 1883, French / Photo © Giancarlo Costa / Bridgeman Images.

Bulk Discounts Available

Children grow closer and closer to eternity every day.
There is no time to waste.

If this book has helped you become a better Catholic parent, please share it with your family and friends.

If you think the families in your parish would benefit from it, please talk to your parish priest about TAN's giveaway program.

Contact:

TAN Books
CustomerService@TANBooks.com

Express your interest in a parish giveaway program or bulk discounts.
Our TAN Team will help make that happen.

May God Bless You and Your Little Ones.